Seeing Like a City

Seeing Like
a City

Ash Amin and Nigel Thrift
Drawings by Katarina Nitsch

polity

First published in 2017 by Polity Press

Polity Press
65 Bridge Street
Cambridge CB2 1UR, UK

Polity Press
350 Main Street
Malden, MA 02148, USA

ISBN-13: 978-0-7456-6425-5 (hardback)
ISBN-13: 978-0-7456-6426-2 (paperback)

A catalogue record for this book is available from the British Library.

Library of Congress Cataloging-in-Publication Data

Names: Amin, Ash, author. | Thrift, N. J., author.
Title: Seeing like a city / Ash Amin, Nigel Thrift.
Description: Cambridge, UK ; Malden, MA : Polity Press, 2016. | Includes
    bibliographical references and index.
Identifiers: LCCN 2016017516 (print) | LCCN 2016029541 (ebook) | ISBN
    9780745664255 (hardcover : alk. paper) | ISBN 0745664253 (hardcover :
    alk. paper) | ISBN 9780745664262 (pbk. : alk. paper) | ISBN 0745664261
    (pbk. : alk. paper) | ISBN 9781509515615 (mobi) | ISBN 9781509515622
    (epub)
Subjects: LCSH: Cities and towns. | Sociology, Urban. | Human geography.
Classification: LCC HT119 .A49 2016 (print) | LCC HT119 (ebook) | DDC
    307.76–dc23
LC record available at https://lccn.loc.gov/2016017516

Typeset in 11 on 13 pt Sabon by Toppan Best-set Premedia Limited
Printed and bound in the UK by Clays Ltd, St. Ives PLC

For further information on Polity, visit our website: politybooks.com

Contents

Acknowledgements

We are very grateful to Katarina Nitsch for agreeing to illustrate this book. Katarina, who draws human and non-human relations in the city, chose ideas in the text she was taken by. We left the choice of ideas and their exact locations to her, as we wanted to add an independent, visual, dimension to the book. We are delighted with the drawings. We also thank the three anonymous referees for their insightful comments on an earlier draft. Thank you too to John Wiley & Sons, Inc. for allowing us to republish parts of the article 'Space', which appears in *The Encyclopedia of Geography: People, the Earth, Environment and Technology*. (Excerpts reprinted with full permission.) Finally, we are indebted to Jan Parsons for painstakingly assembling the book from disparate chapters and bibliographies. The book's title *Seeing Like a City* has been used before, by Mariana Valverde, Saskia Sassen and Warren Magnussen. We borrow it here to encapsulate the worlding done by cities and the challenge to thought and practice posed by the ontology of spatial 'throwntogetherness', Doreen Massey's captivating term for urban process. Doreen, a friend and inspiration, tragically passed away as we were penning the last lines of the book.

Corner

Prologue

I want you to help me to find out what happened to us.
Ballantyne, 2013, p. 15

It takes satellite images and maps of flows to convey a sense
of the world significance of cities. They light up and map
out the densities of settlement, the traffic of inter-urban
flow, and the dependencies of hinterlands near and far on
cities. Meanwhile, less graphic scholarship reveals that a
small number of urban titans now drive world economic
prosperity and creativity, that their elites possess formida-
ble national and transnational power, that states and mili-
tias increasingly target cities for geopolitical advantage,
that human behaviour is shaped in the habits of metropolitan dwelling, and that the history of the Anthropocene is
predominantly the history of urbanization. This research
and scholarship presents cities as forcing houses: centres
of creativity, competitive advantage and human fulfilment
(Glaeser, 2011), as sites of democracy or revolution rekin-
dled (Harvey, 2012; Merrifield, 2013; Douzinas, 2013),
and as 'worldling' sites that set a standard (Roy, 2014). It
finds the urban everywhere, the tentacles of cities sustaining a new era of 'planetary urbanization' (Brenner, 2014)

and inter-urban networks and alliances driving global geo-politics and political economy (Taylor, 2013). This book locates itself in this same genre of writing. But it is also a reconsideration to compensate for a tendency in this genre to erase the territorial in its keenness to emphasize urban globality, or to reduce the new urban centrality to foundational forces such as capital accumulation (Brenner, 2014; Brenner and Schmid, 2015), or the spatial agglomeration of firms, skills and institutions (Storper, 2013; Scott and Storper, 2015; Storper and Scott, 2016). Instead, as a counterweight, the book looks to the agency of another kind of urban assemblage – the effects of things massed together that furnish the world through closely jaxtaposed or interwoven concentrations of humans, technologies and infrastructures providing much of the push. Our argument is that more than just spatial concentration is involved. It is the coming together of overlapping sociotechnical systems that gives cities their world-making power.

Our aim is to get to the 'citiness' of cities; admittedly, a concept as elusive as the 'humanness' of humans, with many possible configurations and arrangements. Cities are spatial radiations that gather worlds of atoms, atmospheres, symbols, bodies, buildings, plants, animals, technologies, infrastructures, and institutions, each with its own mixes, moorings and motilities, each with its own means of trading living, and dying. What form of distillation is possible without violating the character of cities as 'pluriverses', to borrow William James's (1977) phrase? It certainly cannot be one that reduces these pluriverses to systemic imperatives or spatial essences.

Instead, the distillation has to get close to the combinational machinery itself, for example, the summative force of many entities, networks and sociotechnical networks intersecting and colliding with each other (Farias and Bender, 2011; McFarlane, 2011; Lancione 2014; Batty, 2013; Sennett, 2013). This is the kind of synthesis we attempt in this book, focusing in particular on the agency of sociotechnical systems. Building on our earlier book (Amin and

Thrift, 2002), we see the city as a machine whose surge comes from the liveliness of various bodies, materials, symbols, and intelligences held in relation within specific networks of calculation and allocation, undergirded by diverse regimes and rituals of organization and operation. We distil 'citiness' down to the combined vitality and political economy of urban sociotechnical systems, which we believe define the modern city. Together, the arrangements of water, electricity, logistics, communication, circulation and the like, instantiate and sustain life within and beyond cities in all sorts of ways: allocating resource and reward, enabling collective action, shaping social dispositions and affects, marking time, space and map, maintaining order and discipline, sustaining transactions, moulding the environmental footprint. These arrangements are more than a mere 'infrastructural' background, the silent stage on which other powers perform. The mangle of sociotechnical systems in a city is formative in every respect, regardless of its state of sophistication. This, at least, is our thesis.

The project we want to begin in this book is to think again about urban vitality, but this time by understanding both its machinic qualities and the way in which it constantly creates new publics, publics that are new forms of here and there. So, for example, in addressing why and how some cities can be thought of as growth engines, we will decentre familiar accounts that privilege the presence of particular assets such as the concentration of skills and intelligence, firms and institutions, or untraded interdependencies, by focusing on supply infrastructures – the urban machinery that keeps stocks up and moving, capabilities replenished, and services flowing (Chapter 4). Similarly, we will explain the experience and mediation of mass poverty, ever more an urban phenomenon, as a problem of access to the means of survival, regulated by the terms of supply of basic public goods and by the very infrastructures of thought currently in place framing world urban poverty (Chapter 5). In turn, to explain urban social dispositions and affects, we will examine the formative power of hybrids of urban aesthetic, technological intelligence and human dwelling, reworking the meaning of human being (Chapter 3). Finally, we will argue that the energy budgets of city sociotechnical systems and the other metabolisms they sustain lie at the heart of the urban ecological footprint, and the stresses of the Anthropocene in general (Chapter 2).

The sociotechnical systems we wish to consider include first, the metabolic systems that service the city in ways without which collective life would be impossible – water, energy, sanitation, food and so on, each of which forms its own system of provisioning. Second, we want to consider the ways in which the city produces a sense of direction, both as a means of finding a way around an increasingly complex spatial order, and in the way that the city literally directs its inhabitants' lives, allowing them access to, and egress from, some spaces, while simultaneously banning them from others. Third, we want to show how human identities and affects in the city are both coproduced and pumped around, with much of the work done by an urban landscape that has become increasingly sentient. Finally, we want to show how all of this infrastructural activity produces even larger effects. Over time, it mixes all manner of beings together in a way that can genuinely be regarded as evolutionary. The increasing evidence for an Anthropocene bears out the way in which humanity has stamped its footprints on the planet by constructing urban forms that act as carriers for life.

Most books on the city, except those that involve ethnography, tend to start from the outside in; that is, they want to see the city as a whole and map aspects of it, or they want to see the city as an expression of a larger force. In contrast, we want to see the city from the inside out, not because we are looking for a false sense of intimacy but because cities work from the ground up. No matter how open and stretched the city may be, the combination of elements in each city varies in ways that are themselves constitutive, with the many elements of 'infrastructure', without which a city does not exist, becoming not just incidental, but central to how and what cities are: a rough analogy might be that infrastructure is now the urban equivalent of the machinery of breathing. The 'machinic' quality of infrastructure, we wish to argue, drags in all manner of actors, only some of whom are what we might conventionally call human. Without an understanding of this ground-level hum, the city is shorn of a large part of its existence, and the central part of how it is able to reproduce itself as a place. Without this knowledge, we cannot understand the importance that cities have gained in our times, an importance that can only grow as infrastructure becomes ever more pervasive.

Acquiring this knowledge requires making sense of the collectives formed and maintained by sociotechnical networks. It involves following these networks, rather than forcing the variegations at ground level into the received categories of theory or discipline. Generalizations have to derive from the reconstruction of the visible and hidden machinery of urban metabolism and organization, while accepting that they can only be provisional, given that the sociotechnical networks are themselves constantly reworked by their in-built technical and human intelligences. Thinking about the city in this aggregative and experimental way requires intellectual honesty, as we argue in Chapter 1, so that plural methods, intelligences and sensibilities can all be indexed, with the sciences and arts, and designated and lay experts, allowed equal opportunity to narrate the facts and stories of the sociotechnical city. Reconstructing the city ground-up requires making visible its hidden-in-plain-sight infrastructures and disclosing their force and performativity.

This is an important political project. Why? First, because the mix of actors the infrastructure enables is itself an important part of human history, since it is through this mixing that different connections and possibilities become apparent, that different visibilities hove into view, and that different kinds of being can be invented. Second, because each of the tramlines of infrastructure contains its own peculiar forms of cruelty as well as promise. We use the word cruelty knowingly, since we are talking here about machines that legislate who and what lives and who and what dies, and who and what lives in what form. Of course, the city has many infrastructural components, and we will touch on only some of them in this book. But we need to be clear that, in the final analysis, cities are systems for directing and for provisioning life in ways that produce immense combinatorial power and immense constraint. We are convinced that each of these infrastructures has its own pinch points, which themselves constitute political arenas. In other words, the understudied republic that is the infrastructure of the modern city can become the main focus of political action. This is our core argument.

We are talking here about a politics of leverage, a politics of small interventions with large effects, a politics of locating pinch points, and a politics of urban life as a trickster assemblage of like and unlike. Matters of infrastructural tuning and adjustment turn out to be key, whatever the arena. We are talking about what we can make of the commons that we have built ourselves, but continue to reserve for just a few human and nonhuman elites (Heise 2008). In other words, we conclude in favour of an urban politics of fair access to infrastructure – and fair infrastructure – in this book. Other kinds of politics exist, of course, none of which we are devaluing. Instead, we attempt to set out a politics true to the machine that the city is, which is able to convert often quite small interventions into very large gains for the many, without necessarily touching on what some have come to regard as the only available levers of change, whether planning or political party or revolution. We believe that major shifts in life chance really can come from the proto-political stuff of infrastructure, when it is, however briefly, switched into being as a political force. The city is brimful of these moments of opportunity.

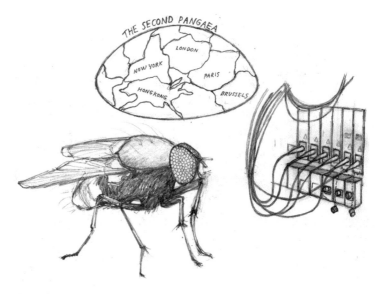

The Second Pangaea

New York · London · Paris · Hong Kong · Brussels

Facet

– 1 –

Looking through the City

We can begin by asking what and where the city is. If cities exist as physical entities, they do so as sprawling miasmas giving rise to all kinds of influence radiating around the world. It is ill conceived to think of them as simply territorial formations, though the instinct to do so remains prevalent. Then, whatever their geography, they remain extraordinarily complex entities – a mangle of machines, infrastructures, humans, nonhumans, institutions, networks, metabolisms, matter and nature – where the coming together is itself constitutive of urbanity and its radiated effects. So, if cities have become world-making, striding out across the world, defining the character of human settlement, giving shape to the transformed nature of the Anthropocene, and providing the main impetus behind political economy (as we argue in this and the next two chapters), how and why this is so is not self-evident. The tendency endures to count factors – the presence or absence of key attributes – rather than to focus on the nature of the combinatorial ecology and how it forces reconsideration of the staples of urban agency and analysis (as explored in this chapter), the dynamic and vulnerabilities of the unfolding 'Anthropocene' (Chapter 2), and the meaning of what it is to be sentient (Chapter 3).

How, then, to assess the character of the city and its
generative powers, which we see as world-making, sociotechnical, and a challenge to a disciplinary heritage when
urban analysis is confined to specialist sub-disciplines such
as urban studies, town and country planning, and architecture or urban design? Or this heritage barely alters its
precepts in light of the hybrid urban processes remak-
ing economy, society, nature, politics and culture. If the
world significance of cities is increasingly acknowledged
in scholarship and policy practice, it has yet to lead to
any rethinking of the fundamentals of core disciplines in
the social sciences. Economics, political science, sociology,
anthropology, and even geography – the most spatial of
these disciplines – have yet to consider how an ontology
formed by urban specificities might require new intra- and
inter-disciplinary composites of thought and method. In
this chapter we argue that understanding cities requires
knowledge practices that are distributed and combinatorial, thus calling into question established disciplinary
and professional legacies. The proposition that knowing
the world might require knowing the city in this way has
barely altered thinking in the mainstream social sciences.

Business trip

Urban World

Let us begin with an audit of the world significance of cities.

First, only a small number of cities drive world economic growth (McKinsey Global Institute, 2012). According to the McKinsey Global Institute, by 2010, six hundred cities, accounting for no more than one fifth of the world's population, were generating 60 per cent of global GDP (Dobbs et al., 2011). They were largely from the North, with 380 of its cities responsible for half of global output. McKinsey calculates that, by 2025, the same number of cities will generate the same volume of GDP, but a third of the constituents from the North will have dropped out, replaced by 136 cities from the emerging economies, primarily from China (100), as well as a dozen or more from India. The top one hundred cities are expected to account for 35 per cent of GDP growth, a group composed of 'middleweight' cities (rather than today's 'megacities'), many again from China and elsewhere in the South, propped up by the know-how and purchasing power of a sizeable new middle class. With the next four hundred cities expected to add only 6 per cent to growth, the world economy will depend on the state of six hundred cities: their quality of infrastructure and services, their ability to manage largely unplanned urban expansion and related problems of congestion, environmental stress and urban maintenance,[1] and their capacity to sustain growth, meet demand and satisfy needs. In other words, the economics of world prosperity will pivot around the supply and distributional conditions that make cities competitive.

Second, this economic might is shored up by other urban concentrations of power. The top-ranking cities, or, more accurately, their central business districts, are massive collections of knowledge, creativity and innovation, political and elite power, cultural and symbolic influence, and financial and infrastructural might. Together, they drive national and international life. Though the exact measure of this power remains elusive (due to nation-biased statistical limitations and because much of it courses under the radar in informal deals, closed boardroom decisions and hidden transactions), rankings of the global influence of individual cities are beginning to circulate. One of these is the A. T. Kearney (2012) Global Cities Index, which measures a city's engagement in business activity (e.g. corporate HQs, top service firms, value of capital markets), human capital formation, information exchange, cultural experience and political influence (e.g. presence of embassies, think-tanks, international organizations). The 2012 ranking, in descending order, lists New York, London, Paris, Tokyo, Hong Kong, Los Angeles, Seoul, Brussels, Washington, Singapore, Sydney, Vienna and Beijing: familiar names fast being chased by many new ones from China and India, according to A. T. Kearney. Linked into common corporate, supply or transactional chains, and sharing elite interests (Khanna, 2011; Taylor, 2004), these cities exercise a network power that circumvents and displaces that exercised by traditional jurisdictions of state and polity, prompting Saskia Sassen (2012a: 5) to aver that 'our geopolitical future...will be determined in good part through twenty or so strategic worldwide urban networks'. The state-centred discourses and tools of political science will need to change in order to grasp this nodal/network power (Taylor, 2013).

Third, these economic and political powers are neither mirrored equitably across the urban landscape, nor do they provide assurance of wellbeing within cities. In fact, they are part of a fabric of extreme inter-urban and intra-urban disparity. By 2050, 70 per cent of the world's expected nine billion people will be living in urban areas, a relentless rise from today's 50 per cent (UN-Habitat, 2008). Today there are over 450 cities with more than one million inhabitants, and they include twenty-one cities with between ten and 35 million people. The pace of growth is particularly marked in the developing world, whose cities – stretched in every respect – are projected to house 80 per cent of the world's urban population in 2030. Already by 2020, a billion of these residents are expected to be living in slums (ibid.). These ill-serviced and very often officially ignored or condemned settlements are set to become part of the normal urban landscape. They are zones of extreme poverty, marginality and deprivation, and day-to-day survival in an informal economy amounting to half the world's workforce of 1.8 billion people (expected to rise to two-thirds by 2020), according to the OECD (Jütting and de Laiglesia, 2009). In other words, in the contemporary city profoundly divided social worlds are co-located on a very large scale, with power and resources biased towards the elites and middle classes at the expense of poor majorities. This spatiality of extremes co-located and disparities amplified is still inadequately understood by all the social sciences interested in the dynamics of social differentiation and inequality.

Fourth, global environmental change is powered by, and is largely about, urban metabolism. As Burdett and Rode (2011, p. 10) observe, 'occupying less than 2 per cent of the earth's surface, urban areas concentrate...between 60 and 80 per cent of global energy consumption, and approximately 75 per cent of CO_2 emissions'. Their energy demands are vast and ever-growing, as are their emissions, although the environmental footprints of individual cities vary considerably: 'whereas cities in Europe, the US and Brazil, for example, have a lower environmental impact than their respective countries, cities in India and China have a much larger impact owing to their significantly higher income levels compared with national averages (op. cit., p. 11)'. The hazards of climate change, in contrast, are confronting all cities with punitive energy and food prices, weather extremes, flash floods and coastal erosions, vulnerable or failing infrastructures, debilitating levels of pollution and congestion, and a host of other risks and vulnerabilities. The close reciprocities between urban footprints and climate change, forced evolution towards a new wild (Pearce, 2015), and a generalized 'onto-cartography' in which nonhuman agencies have their say (Bryant, 2014), as discussed more fully in the next chapter, are generally underestimated in writing on climate change and environmental vulnerability. But, at the very least, the better management of urban metabolism, for example, through spatial infill, smart infrastructures, waste recycling and combined energy, might prove to be more critical for securing the future of the earth than hitherto imagined (IPCC, 2012; Institute for the Future, 2012; Lindsay, 2010).

Fifth, and paradoxically, the new urban centrality comes with no commensurate increase in the power of municipal authorities. The world over, city governments are hampered by fiscal and juridical constraints, are often captured by vested interests or held back by shortages of resource, capability or commitment, while national governments – with far greater powers and resources – often remain largely blind to urban centrality. In turn, any attempt to bolster municipal governance, for example, the World Bank's (2009) effort to get national governments to benchmark their policies through cities and to increase municipal powers, still confronts powerful nongovernmental forces with different designs on the urban. These include business coalitions for which cities are only transactional nodes, urban elites commandeering urban assets for themselves, various systems of provisioning and intelligence lying beyond public scrutiny and control, and illegal networks wresting the wrong kind of possibility from urban scarcity. If the world is run out of cities, it is with municipal authorities playing an adjunct role, dependent on alliances that compromise their autonomy and authority. Indeed, in recent decades, some city governments pressed by rising costs, falling central government subsidy, and fiscal constraints, have entered into interest-rate swaps with global investment banks to raise bond revenue, a form of speculative hedging that has left them saddled with crippling debt and empty coffers during the current financial crisis (Sassen, 2014).

Shoe tossing

Urbanicity

These symptoms of the urban age raise important questions about the nature of the dynamic of life compressed
into, and run out of, two per cent of the earth's surface,
a dynamic that may have something to do with understanding the 'throwntogether' ontology of the city (Massey,
2005). This is an ontology of many kinds of gravitational
force juxtaposed: metabolic networks, infrastructures and
built forms, technical systems and institutions, diverse
structures of authority, power and intelligence. This spatiality may be generative in its own right, as intimated
by writing on the combinations of elite power, organized authority and social rights in global cities (Sassen,
2006); on the concentration of knowledge, sociality and
interdependent firms in the economically most dynamic

cities (Glaeser, 2011; Storper, 2013); on the sustenance and resilience provided by well-maintained and evenly distributed urban infrastructures (Graham and Marvin, 2001; Heynen, Kaïka and Swyngedouw, 2006; Amin, 2014a); and on the social webs of improvisation that enable survival in cities organized solely for the well-off (Simone, 2010; Venkatesh, 2014).

This ontology has been the focus of a 'relational' turn in urban studies in recent years imagining cities as a combinatorial force field (Amin and Thrift, 2002; Amin, 2007; McFarlane, 2011a; Farías, 2011; Simone, 2011; Taylor, 2013). Here the city is thought of as a 'complex adaptive assemblage' (Dovey, 2010; 2012) governed by the balance of force between many authority structures – corporate and institutional, technical and infrastructural, computational and cartographic, social and symbolic, codified and informal. The city is not seen as reducible to imperatives of base or superstructure, or to the self-organizing dynamic of an open system (Batty, 2005; Sanders, 2008). Instead, the relational approach delves into the push and pull of competing hybrids of association, explicitly seeking to understand how their 'traffic, exchanges, and interactions' (Ong, 2009, p. 88) maintain particular orders and hierarchies of power (McFarlane, 2011b; Graham, 2010; Weizman, 2012). The labour involved is explicitly recognized, as are the many formal and informal entities of the force field (from commanding ideas, people, policies and institutions to mundane directionalities of urban design, engineering and calculation). Urban force is conceptualized as distributed, coalitional and heterogeneous, and as fixed through various returns of power but also as constantly evolving in new directions because of the emergent properties of interactive systems.

It is this kind of urban force – combinatorial and disjunctive – that is likely to be involved in generating the outcomes listed in the preceding section, not one of particular presences; for example, the number of entrepreneurs, leaders and mediators, the synergies between bureaucracies, corporations and research organizations, or the smartness and speed of sociotechnical systems. Urban agency may be a function both of how, in a force field of relational interactions, hybrid inputs are aligned and made to work through various coupling and amplification devices (e.g. infrastructures, bureaucracies, calculative logics), and of the character of the general ecology of interactions (e.g. tolerance capacity, population dynamics, flow turbulence). The field and its rules of operability, rather than its individual entities, may matter most in explaining collective urban agency, operating as a practical capability and intelligence spread across intersecting infrastructures. This intersection can be thought of as the machine, habitat and atmosphere of the city, one that holds things in place, enables process, and endows the entities and their associations with purposeful capacity.

Let us take one world-making capacity as an example: the special character of urban intelligence, which is normally reduced in the literature to the presence of particular types of people, skills and dispositions. Yet, this intelligence, be it the creativity necessary to enable search and innovation or the social detachment that helps urbanites to negotiate the city's many demands and sensations, cannot be reduced to particular types of human or social attribute, because in the city objects, technologies and infrastructures are the prosthetics that enable subjects to think, act and feel (Amin, 2012; Gandy, 2005; Jacobs, 2012). These prosthetics are on the inside of human being, and when on the outside, for example, as 'smart' buildings and infrastructures, they are anything but inert. The assemblages of machinery, technological intelligence and matter play as much more than just a valet service to deciding human beings. They enable collective urban life through their provisions and circulations, and they are the envelopes in which humans enact their personal and social lives in the city (Mackenzie, 2010; Thrift, 2012; Shepard, 2011).

This is not to reduce the city to machine intelligence, in the way of a new literature on 'smart cities' fed by a fantasy of computational systems successfully working on data from sensors lodged in every pore of the city so as to produce a delirium of choice. Rather, it is to acknowledge the interactive intelligence of the provisioning infrastructures, built forms and associational networks, and their reciprocities with thinking and acting humans. In cities awash with sensors and processors nested in street technologies, public infrastructures, buildings, homes and offices, and all kinds of mobile device, it is undeniable that calculations in 'code/space' (Kitchin and Dodge, 2011) continuously adjust the urban habitat without active human intervention (Khan, 2011). In this environment 'imbued with the capacity to remember, correlate and anticipate', as Mark Shepard (2011) observes, we are on 'the cusp of a near-future city capable of reflexively monitoring its environment and our behaviour within it, becoming an active agent in the organization of everyday life' (p. 10). But it is an active agency that both reconfigures and enrols human being itself, as we argue more fully in Chapter 3.

Immersed in an intelligent habitat, urban dwellers, including experts and decision makers, are constantly stretched beyond their bodies by adjunct nonhumans, enacting their subjectivity through the interdependencies so formed (Ash, 2013). Typically, circulating with smartphones that offer a personalized map, and images, sounds and conversations that mingle with those of the city, they navigate the city as a series of dots and pins, their subjectivity formed in the intersections of personal biography, urban experience and wireless dwelling (Mackenzie, 2010; Born, 2013). They find themselves immersed in multiple fields of intelligence with 'their own kinds of vitality, capacities of repetition, variation and adaption, that in turn feed back into the becomings of sentience' (Fuller, 2011, p. 181). As one of us has argued elsewhere, in the smart city, 'a new kind of inhabitant who can don the city like a cloak' is formed, joining other 'avatars, at least in the sense that the persona they don can be expressed in more dimensions' (Thrift, 2012, p. 159).

This immersive subjectivity and distributed intelligence is not just a feature of the technologically mediated urban environment. It is often assumed that in cities with rudimentary technologies, poor infrastructures and failing bureaucracies, where humans are left to do the heavy lifting, inhabitants proceed without prosthetics, challenged rather than formed by their habitat. Rarely in writing on the world's urban majority living in challenging circumstances does the habitat feature on the inside of subjectivity. Slums, suburbs, congested public spaces, tower blocks and busy city centres tend to get narrated as uncongenial spaces that urban dwellers learn to negotiate or survive, distorting subjectivity from the outside, for example, by encouraging opportunistic, feral or furtive behaviour. In contrast, a new genre of urban ethnography is emerging, showing that humans are equally of their habitat in these environments, with agency very much a hybrid of mind, body, machine and matter. Thus, technologies are revealed to be woven into daily sociality in even the most makeshift of places, in the form of the rub of machine, building material and body in cramped space, pirated technologies providing essential services, mundane objects that enable connectivity, and hope sustained by consumer or educational technologies (see Sundaram, 2010 for Delhi; Simone, 2014a for Jakarta; Pieterse and Simone, 2014 for various African cities). Social behaviour here is as materially mediated as it is in the software-dominated city, if only for the simple reason that in every urban setting, 'built environments engage their users' (Degen and Rose, 2012, p. 3273) as 'perceptual memories that mediate the present moment of experience...by multiplying, judging and dulling the sensory encounter' (p. 3271).

These ethnographies suggest that the reciprocities of habitat and subjectivity are ubiquitous, and not just confined to fringe spaces such as abandoned parks or parking lots, where unusual plant and animal species may cohabit with visiting humans, themselves dwelling in these spaces in unusual ways (Gandy, 2012). Nor are they confined

to orphan spaces such as cemeteries, where urban out-
casts often live close to, and with the ground, enabling
them to improvise, make ends meet, hone a degree of
environmental awareness, and build cloaked occult identities as skills of survival (cf. de Boeck and Plissart, 2004,
on Kinshasa's street-children and Sawhney, 2009, on the
noir in Delhi's poor neighbourhoods). Thus, for example,
Charles Hirschkind (2006) shows how taped sermons in
the streets of Cairo form a sensorium for ethical reflection
amid the frenzy of the city. Silwa and Riach (2012) reveal
how smells of disinfectant, boiled cabbage or perfume in
the public spaces of Krakow serve as mnemonics of association – positive or negative – with Poland's communist
past or its future in the European Union. Elijah Anderson
(1999) shows how the 'codes of the street' that equip
people in Philadelphia's high-risk neighbourhoods with a
'careful way of moving, of acting, of getting up and down
the streets' (p. 23) are an iteration between honed instinct
and street syntax (e.g. signals sent out by gathered groups
of people, cars slowing down, dark and unkempt corners –
see also Swanton, 2010; Blokland, 2008; Goffman, 2014;
Venkatesh, 2014). Sara Fregonese (2012) uncovers how
street atmospheres incorporating gunfire, eerie silences,
barriers, hasty movement, partisan banners and flags, play
their part in the geopolitics of fear and anxiety in the
conflict-ridden city of Beirut. These examples confirm Simmel's (2002, p. 17) prescient observation a century ago,
that a 'person does not end with the limits of his physical
body or with the area to which his physical activity is
immediately confined, but embraces, rather, the totality of
meaningful effects which emanates from him temporally
and spatially'. The urban landscape, as sensorium, habitat
and directional intelligence, can be thought of as a space
of 'outstincts' and 'escalated atmospheres' (Thrift, 2014)
stretching bodily instincts and intelligences.

   In this discussion on the infrastructures of urban agency,
we have focused on just one example – the hybrids of
urban intelligence and social subjectivity. But as we show

Hurried

in the chapters that follow, similar sociotechnical combinations lie behind other forms of urban push, inviting
analysis of the dynamics of prosperity and poverty that
note how the composition and political economy of a
city's sociotechnical systems convert, amplify, and distribute resources, and produce the power to acknowledge the
enrolments of the built form (e.g. the symbolic power of
iconic buildings, the silent allocations of infrastructures),
to change the calculus of global hazard and risk.

Knowing the City

This machinic agency defies a science of fixed structures
and assumptions, for its powers are simultaneously struc-
tural and relational, recursive and emergent. It requires
a science able to get close to situated interactions, urban
processes that transcend disciplinary boundaries, and the
agency of sociotechnical systems. In the main, thinking in
this direction has tended to veer towards the ideographic,
towards ethnographies that honour heterogeneities that
defy levelling generalizations and systemic abstractions.
Reasoning has proceeded from cases (Becker, 2014), with
the best of the genre stopping short of the parochial by
weaving in the strictures of general principles – say of
market, political economy and planning – without over-
shadowing the idiographic (partly by treating these strictures as immanent rather than totalizing). The cases have
experimented with hyphenated concepts such as 'pirate
modernity' (Sundaram, 2010), 'improvised formality'
(Simone, 2011) or 'knot rhythms' (De Boeck, 2014) to
get at the intricacies of the general and the specific involved
in city making. They have found a way of capturing the
thrown and held togetherness of urban life.

   However, all that said, these ethnographies reveal little
about aggregate urban dynamics – the city as the sum of
its assemblages (Pieterse, 2013, for example, laments such
a gap in explaining Africa's 'rogue' urbanism). One answer

has come from complexity science, likening cities to adaptive systems regulated by their combined pluralities and interactions (Batty, 2005). Here, as Sanders (2008, p. 276) argues, cities are conceived as 'dynamic systems where the variables (people, businesses, governments, etc.) are constantly interacting and changing – for better or worse – in response to each other, creating nonlinear feedback loops that either promote or deplete the life energy upon which their futures depend. As complex adaptive systems, [cities] are organized, coherent entities in which physical conditions, decisions, perceptions, and the social order are constantly changing.' The challenge set for urban analysis is to identify the feedback mechanisms and model aggregate effects so that the balances of recursion and rupture can be calculated.

The exponents of complexity science believe such calculation is finally possible because of advances in data capture and analysis offering live data feeds on all manner of urban phenomena from digital sensors everywhere in the city, sophisticated software to map the typologies and topologies of interaction and aggregation, and modelling techniques capable of processing large data and multiple variables without eliminating ambiguity, uncertainty and emergence. They believe that advancements in data capture, computational modelling and nonlinear science now allow the living city to be constructed and tracked in its plural and hidden detail, simulated in ways that allow the underlying dynamics to be understood and potentially worked upon (Batty, 2013). If, until recently, quantitative science in urban studies might have suffered from the criticism of being distant from reality and process, its systems science cousin claims the ability to stay close to specificity and nuance in the way of qualitative science, but also to capture and interpret the aggregates.

These are seductive claims for city leaders confronted by an increasingly opaque, hazardous and uncertain urban environment, yet still expected to make informed, judicious and effective decisions. What better than a science able to work with the urban as a field of interactions and feedback loops, offering planning choices cognisant of field dynamics? And indeed, where funds, technologies and expertise permit, municipal authorities have rushed to establish or fund intelligence units collecting and analysing large datasets, visualizing the city of flows, interactions and feedback loops, identifying the forces of recursion, amplification and dissonance, developing realistic scenarios with the help of probabilistic models and sophisticated simulation technologies, and drawing on real-time data analysis to fine-tune policy making. Such moves are helping urban decision makers to think that the city made legible by complexity science is the basis of knowing and governing the city as an open, plural system.

It is an open question whether complexity science can actually get close to the city of multitudinous interactions and improvisations that still defy data capture and mathematical modelling, however sophisticated (Townsend, 2013). What we can be sure of is the seduction of access to the urban totality without totalization reducing the ones on policy makers to enrol other methods and insights, especially as pressing circumstances demand quick and unambiguous decisions (jettisoning even the error-bar caveats of complexity science). 'Smart city' ventures premised upon large datasets, ubiquitous software and computational modelling – for example, fully wired new settlements such as Masdar City in Abu Dhabi or Songdo International Business District near Seoul – quickly forget the value of plural and reflexive intelligence, as the flows of raw and worked data between smart monitoring systems thicken into a form of self-referencing technological intelligence. So, it is not the new urban science, which sees itself as anything but formulaic, that may be at fault, but decision makers succumbing to computational intelligence, and in the process losing sight of the city as more than a simple quantum whose recursions, novelties and ambiguities require other forms of intelligence (Greenfield, 2013).

An expanded field of urban intelligence would help to reign in robotic tendencies disguised as neutral techno-intelligence, by directing new technologies to 'focus more on coordination than on command' (Sennett, 2012, p. 76) and by preventing the slippage of urban monitoring from 'sensorship' to censorship (Sassen, 2012b). It would acknowledge intelligences already at work in the city, address situated problems and set urban governance as a challenge of harnessing this plurality rather than subjugating it to a master intelligence. It would recognize the many ways in which urban knowledge is acquired and maintained, including learning and cognition, sensory and bodily perception, conversation and storytelling, memory and archive, formal and informal expertise, symbolic and computational intelligence. It would consider the possibility that it is the spectrum of distributed intelligence that holds the complex city together, prevents it from paralysis or implosion, provides the means of negotiating urban multiplicity, and tests the wisdom of generic urban knowledge management schemes.

We would suggest that to know the complex city is to draw on this broader spectrum instead of privileging experts and models. Otherwise the centripetal and monitory tendencies of computational governance will persist, while the city of many logics and happenings continues to evolve in nonlinear and unplanned ways, but with the city's functioning knowledges kept in the shadows. A first step towards the city of ubiquitous intelligence would be to treat computational intelligence as part of the wider labour of valorizing different knowledges and placing them in agonistic tension so as to collectively validate governance decisions. This is no easy matter, given that many knowledge practices are hidden, informal, improvisatory, or embedded in the urban machinery. There is no knowledge parliament to manage this heterogeneity.

However, some principles of knowledge management can be tabled. One is the value of maintaining a network of local centres of intelligence drawing on different combinations of lay, technical and professional expertise to address local matters of concern, eventually feeding into citywide deliberative networks. Cultivating pools of situated knowledge and harnessing them to address citywide challenges in a deliberative manner would become an explicit governance aim. Another, relatedly, would be to take steps to open a city's centres of strategic decision making to multiple methods of analysis and to greater public scrutiny, so that calculative technologies, findings and recommendations themselves can become objects of debate and external validation. Similarly, there should be ample space for a counter-culture of urban intelligence and planning, so that alternative designs can flourish and eventually press delegated authorities to justify their decisions. These are principles of urban management based on public audit, collaborative judgement and heterogeneous expertise, working across a landscape of distributed intelligence in order to address the routine, the unexpected and the strategic.

These principles belong to a structure of knowing slowed down to allow for measured judgement (Hall, 2012), even in the face of immediate problems that inevitably tempt authorities to act impulsively. They require careful thought from the authorities about the locations and sociotechnical sources of urban expertise, about how much of the city can be known and governed, about appropriate methods of measurement and calculation, and about the basis – evidential, discursive and ethical – on which decisions should be made (Helbing, 2009). They imply that finding a way through a complex and evolving urban environment requires decision makers to think carefully about the baselines of urban expertise, including the value of computational knowledge, and about the value of engaging others in finding solutions in uncertain and contested knowledge circumstances (Callon et al., 2009; Krebs, 2011). They nudge actors reliant on panoptical vision to concede to multiple methods, partial insights and hybrids of human and nonhuman intelligence, to settle for a modest and open 'science' of urban knowing, to question canons of thought that pretend access to the hidden depths of the city.

This alternative science of the city learns how to scan the knowledge horizon in order to seek out and enjoin expert artefacts, people and institutions and to harness machine intelligence for the common good. It concerns itself with making visible, rather than taking for granted, the hidden work of algorithms, machines and codes behind the city's many sociotechnical systems and their effects, so as to make the city fabric a heuristic space in which publics can engage with machine intelligence (Sassen, 2012b, p. 74). It looks to redesign the affective resonances of machine intelligence so that new public demands can arise (e.g. by planting sensors on trees or buildings that can express environmental stress in the form of cries or tears, or by visualizing the city's resource, information and metabolic flows so that maldistributions and pinch points can be identified and addressed – cf. Shepard, 2011). Here urban science itself becomes involved in shifting 'attention from the material constitution of subjects and forms of democracy to more explicit deployments of objects, settings and devices in the organization of participation (see Marres and Lezaun, 2011, p. 496). It commits, even in the most urgent situations, to working horizontally across diverse sources – maps, archives, simulations, numbers, surveys, ethnographies, mnemonic clues, imaginaries and narratives[2] – relying on skills of assembly, negotiation, collaboration.

This kind of urban smartness begins with the very precepts of urban knowing, before resorting to new tools of data capture and new armies of detached expertise. It prises open the closed circuits of authority, putting them to the test of polyvocality and constitutive uncertainty, knowing that the city can only be known partially, provisionally and experimentally, its combinatorial ontology defying authority reliant on an all-knowing and governing centre. It looks to harness, as Mariana Valverde (2011, p. 308) argues, the 'logic of nuisance [that] has by no means been eliminated by the modernist habit', accepting that even the most legislated of cities remains governed by 'both subjective offensiveness and objective, general rules, and there is no reason to think that one will drive out the other: It may be...that "seeing like a city" is precisely a combination of heterogeneous ways of governing that may appear to be contradictory when examined philosophically but which, in practice, supplement and/ or replace each other without fanfare' (Valverde, 2011, p. 308). Perhaps the truth of the heterotopic city is that such ways of knowing and governing are not even philosophically contradictory.

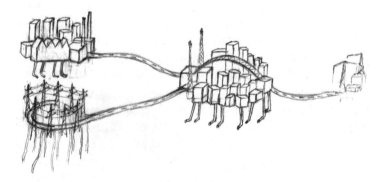

Infrastructure

Conclusion

An obvious question is whether this way of proceeding measures up to the challenges of twenty-first-century urbanism with which we opened the chapter. Critics will argue that with so much in the world shaped by what goes on in just two per cent of the earth's surface (from the differentials of wealth and wellbeing and the trends of world culture, politics and economic change, to the pace and consequences of global warming), cities need to be centrally managed in ways that directly tackle the drivers of change. They will argue that knowledge pluralism and urban government are not the same, and that the former should be harnessed by the authorities to roll out firm policies to reduce carbon emissions, to harness the power of the richest cities, to link economic growth to social cohesion and environmental stewardship, to ensure government efficiency and transparency.

But, can this be done against a background of de facto governance that includes interest-biased government, pervasive clientelism, fiscal deficit and unfettered market rule in many parts of the world? Advocates of 'seeing like a state' will argue that these are problems to be tackled and not just accepted, and best tackled from a vaulting vantage point floating above the fray of the living city, unhampered by the nuances of urban process or complex thinking. Leaving aside who occupies this vantage point, this thinking fits into a long tradition of programmatic urban planning in the image of the idea, its projects designing the large-scale engineering of housing, industry, recreation, circulation, maintenance and repair, and welfare. The logic of intervention has been to mould – perhaps bludgeon is the more correct term – rather than work with underlying dynamics and feedback loops. But with scale as the measure of achievement, the results have to be judged as impressive, though often tarnished by the brute force of central urban planning. Citing such achievements, the logic of 'seeing like a state' might at best concede an adjunct role to the logic of 'seeing like a city', looking to it for additional intelligence for central authorities, or for relief for communities left out of the prospectus.

The problem with this mode of reasoning is that the urban ontology and grounded epistemology that we have traced out alters the very meaning of authority, towards one of adjusting the means rather than the minutiae of daily urban life (e.g. of ensuring general access to services, housing, income, public space), of finding a way through heterogeneity, rather than rolling a blueprint over it (Kornberger, 2012). In a heterotopic field – the contemporary city – the centre is radically displaced, pressed to steer without suppressing the many knowledge practices and organizational vernaculars: politically, by arbitrating disputes, aligning interests and designs with diverse publics; and practically, by ensuring that the machinery of general provisioning – food, water, energy, shelter, education, healthcare, transport, communication – works for the city as a whole. It provides a nudge towards a *politics of traction*, as we illustrate in the second half of the book.

The challenges posed by 'seeing like a city' extend to the premises of scholarship itself. They require the disciplines – social and physical – interested in cities to reconsider settled conventions, to pass through an 'indisciplinary' (Taylor, 2013) first step to acknowledge hybrids of spatial process that disrupt the inherited categories of state-based measurement, the artificial boundaries of individual disciplines, and clear distinctions of cause and effect, model and manifestation, human and nonhuman, reason and unreason. They suggest as a second step a unified science comfortable with heterogeneous tools and rationalities in order to piece together an evolving open system by staying as close to the ground of process itself. This is a science of trial and error, continuous revision and joint intelligence, designed to sift through the interdependencies of markets and modes of calculation, of weather, industry and infrastructure, of body, technology and sociality, of the myriad spatial forms that intersect in the city. It becomes a meeting place where scholarship moves past general principles and disciplinary precepts towards artful reconstruction of actual modes of existence through forensic retracing, hybrid precepts, and skills of disciplinary reconciliation (Latour, 2013).

That means seeing the world as a constellation of existential assemblages, each requiring ideas, tools, and sensibilities that do justice to their own integrity, rather than to some fiction of a universal standard or objective method. It means learning to be diplomatic – knowing how to compare and reconcile modes of machinic being and thinking that are taken to be equally valid – and developing situated forensic skills – the 'step-by-step', thread-by-thread tracing of the various *networks*, and the 'various *trajectories* of veridiction or malediction, each defined by a separate *preposition*. To understand any situation whatsoever is at once to unfold its network and define its preposition, the interpretive key in which it has to be grasped' (Latour, 2013: 66, emphasis in original). This is a science of reconstruction and verification, not of formulas and proofs, but of conjecture. It is a science of different nervous systems. It is a science of incompleteness, of learning what is there over and over again. Most of all, it is a science that recognizes that

> Many machines – especially those of the social and organic variety – might strive to transform their machinic parts into docile bodies but this forever remains an ideal never fulfilled in practice. There are always subterranean plots, machinic intrigues, tiny acts of treason, and furtive acts of disobedience among parts. Far from being something to be eradicated, these failures of perfect ordering are part of the creativity of machinic being. (Bryant, 2014, p. 81)

An uncertain and uncontrollable science-art. Amen to that, as the saying goes.

Mirror

− 2 −

Shifting the Beginning:
The Anthropocene

It may seem impossible to imagine that a technologically advanced society could choose, in essence, to destroy itself but that is what we are now in the process of doing.

> Kolbert, 2015, p. 189

They say that Gothic novels came into being because science and eighteenth-century rationalism were threatening to empty the world of any romance, spirituality or caprice. Two hundred years later the planet is full of technology but utterly irrational. And I don't feel any need for Gothic excitement.

> Parks, 2014, p. 252 (used by permission of
> W. W. Norton & Company, Inc.)

The real problem is that climate – or the environment more generally – holds us hostage at the same time as it asks for our help.

> Sparrow, 2013, p. 81

Infrastructure begat circulation begat the city begat the Anthropocene.

That is the theme of this chapter. It pursues our thesis that the city is an infrastructural entanglement with considerable formative agency by showing that cities are one of the main products and producers of the Anthropocene. By this, we do not mean cities are a stable point radiating an urban essence but, instead, recurring moments in the constant rendition and circulation of people and things, moments in which circulation and city constantly reinforce each other in sometimes lasting and sometimes temporary alignments within a 'geologic now' (Ellsworth and Kruse, 2013).

In certain ways, that story of motility is a stock refrain of geographers. Most cities were originally sited at the confluence of trade routes of one form or another, in places that could service, sell and transport agricultural goods. But then, of course, cities themselves became producers of goods as well as state and religious nodes. But we will put an extra twist in the tail by arguing that this rudimentary circulation gradually led to the laying down of 'infrastructure' – a word first coined in French in the 1870s, which subsequently moved into English usage in the 1920s (Gandy, 2014) – on such a scale that it has changed the planet, producing a world in which infrastructure is no longer an effect but a cause. In turn, the multiple layerings of infrastructure have led directly on to the formation of a geological era, which has come to be known as the Anthropocene: the reshaping of the earth by force of human occupation on a sufficient scale that it can be recognized as a separate geological epoch. In this epoch it can be argued that cities are the true planetary citizens, hive entities sharing responsibility for the earth (Vince, 2014). This acceleration is in many different ways about the extension and subsequent deepening of infrastructure in its multiple forms.

Infrastructure, by our account, does not refer simply to actual physical lineaments. It is also, on one level, caught up with the moments of standardization, technical compatibility, professional rivalry, bureaucratic imperatives, regulatory competences and general dispositions which allow things, quite literally, to fit together and, on another level, with the different practices of maintenance and repair which allow infrastructure to continue working in at least some form,[1] which continue to guarantee presence. In other words, coherence is hard won and never assured. But if it can be won, a certain logic of governance can follow, at least for a while, in which form and action are inter-related, one far-removed from familiar legislative and other declarative processes but just as potent (Easterling, 2014a; Valverde, 2015). In other words, infrastructure is a structure of contact that also defines what shows up as real at any juncture. It is the gross material of materiality.

In making such an account of infrastructure and the Anthropocene, we will tread some delicate lines. In particular, we will try to avoid falling over the line between genuine and sometimes horrified concern about a world in which every last sliver of natural habitat seems to be under siege into simple doomsaying and equally the line between an appreciation of some of the wonders of 'the human age' (Ackerman, 2014) and a kind of reverse science fiction

Travel

in which the present is described as an age of humanly wrought technological miracles which will inevitably and by extension produce an eco-modernism which will ride to the rescue of the human and indeed everything else on the planet. As Hamilton, Bonneuil and Gemenne (2015, p. 11) argue, the priority now is neither of these nostrums. Rather, it is 'to extend our ability to think and act beyond human experience'.

Shifting the Beginning: The Second Pangaea

Conventionally, cities have been regarded as the product of the Agricultural Revolution that occurred many thousands of years ago. The surpluses of food produced by cultivating wheat, maize or rice – and the food demands of domesticated livestock – allowed cities to come into existence. They produced writing and the outbursts of written creativity that we now take for granted like plays and new forms of music, they produced state bureaucracies complete with files and surveillance, they produced trade with fixed transactions at fixed sites, they produced merchants – and priests and artisans and bookkeepers, they produced monumental architecture, and they produced systematic ways of living together like streets and public gathering spaces and rooftops. It is even argued that they produced the time to allow abstract thought like mathematics.

But cities produced downsides too. For example, it has been argued that settled agriculture was a disaster for the human race. Jared Diamond (2013) has certainly asserted that the agriculture that allowed cities to flourish initially was a catastrophic mistake from which our bodies have never recovered: average height declined by two to three inches, teeth decayed as grain diets bit, epidemic diseases spiralled, and living in close proximity to livestock and to each other allowed new diseases to flourish and kill.

On this admittedly contested account, it then took thousands of years for the human body to recover – it was not until the twentieth century that Europeans regained the same height as cavemen – and by then a host of new 'evolutionary mismatch' problems had arisen like obesity, hypertension, various kinds of cancer, heart disease, type 2 diabetes and fatty liver disease, all of which stem from the fact that the jumble of genetic and epigenetic adaptations in our mainly Stone Age bodies and our contemporary lifestyles are radically out of synch, so producing greater longevity but also increasing levels of chronic noninfectious disease: 'most of the diseases that affect you are triggered or intensified by environmental factors that have mostly become common since farming or industrialization' (Lieberman, 2013, p. 173). In other words, nearly all of these medical problems were set in train in the time when agriculture first gained ascendancy and cities first came on the scene and were then made worse by subsequent waves of urbanization.

Whatever the exact case, it is clear that the agricultural revolution has gradually produced a second 'dysevolutionary' human being genetically both of and not of the Stone Age world from which it was originally born as the Anthropocene has taken shape. This is an Anthropocene which has, in large part, depended on the construction of an urban realm dependent on food sources which are only partly suited to the human constitution.

At the same time, because of these dietary changes and greater mobility, mixing has begun to occur at the genetic level, probably at an accelerated level of change because of the demography of cities (Cochran and Harpending, 2009), although it is these relatively slow-moving genetic markers which remain the level of existence that seem to be most obdurate to cities' and infrastructure's powers of catalysis. At other levels, however, more rapid change is often in evidence, at times when it might be thought that change would be slowest. Let's consider each of these levels in turn.

To begin with, at the level where it might be thought that there would be the least impact – the geologic – humankind has moved vast amounts of rock and soil and produced numerous new materials in ways which have etched a permanent detrivorous mark on the geological record: the rocks are now scored and scarred by human activity, the soil is a record of disturbance. Cities and their associated infrastructure have acted as the equivalent of a meteorite strike in the extent of their impact on the earth. Geography was often thought to be an offshoot of geology. But no longer. The two have leached into each other in numerous ways. Human beings have begun to change the planet to such a degree that they have started to create their own geological epoch by building one vast ants' nest which extends both down into the ground and up into the air. When an alien explorer looks back at the earth from millions of years in the future, it will be able to discern a recognizable stratum based on the remains of human habitation, not just buildings but all manner of objects and even some kinds of clothes – which will no doubt be interpreted as external coverings periodically discarded as they grow too tight to fit a growing organism (Zalasiewicz, 2009). There may even be direct marks like footprints.

Then there will be concrete, steel and stone, pipes, cables, boreholes and the like. Then iron and steel and plastic and glass and tile. Then nuclear waste. Then all kinds of associated despoliation and especially the trawling of the seabeds. Though human cities may not yet be quite as impressive as biological cities like coral reefs in their scale and longevity, still humanity is catching up fast and will undoubtedly leave a lasting geological legacy of man-made rock and fossils, a kind of urban aggregate made up of materials dislocated and mixed together as a relocated recomposition (Zalasiewicz, 2009). Such comparisons may seem overly dramatic until the sheer planet-shaping amount of energy that human beings now bring to the party is brought into the equation. To give a point of comparison, the earth receives 170,000 terawatts from the sun (Morton, 2009). The primary production of the biosphere via photosynthesis is 130 terawatts. The flux of energy from the centre of the earth is about forty terawatts. Our global civilization is powered by around thirteen terawatts of man-made energy arising mainly from the unprecedented levels of energy consumption associated with cities. The point is that human beings already act as an energy source that begins to compare with plate tectonics in its magnitude and force, although whether the harvesting of the earth's resources that underlies such figures is in reality something akin to an enormous unnatural Ponzi scheme remains a moot point. As Smil (2013, pp. 223–4) puts it, taking in just the energy harvested from the biosphere, all of this 'would have been impossible without greatly expanded claims on the biosphere's photosynthetic productivity, without rising harvests of cultivated and wild phytomass and without increasing contributions of animal foods produced by hunting wild mammals, birds, and fishes'.

Then there is the climatic. The geological record will also show other marks and, most particularly, climate change and mass extinctions. Humans have undoubtedly begun to change the chemical composition of the atmosphere. In the atmosphere, carbon dioxide levels are 50 per cent higher than the Holocene mean. We can be almost uncannily accurate about when this process first started: 1784, when carbon from coal-fired industry began to be deposited worldwide. We also know the exact date when this process accelerated: 1945, when radioactive material began to be laid down after Hiroshima and Nagasaki. The effects of climate change are all too obvious from receding glaciers through storm frequency and violence and associated flooding to warming oceans and a parallel sea-level rise which might reach as high as thirty feet per century. Deserts are spreading too.

Next in degree of change are plants. Trees, for example, can live for hundreds of years, eating the sun (Morton, 2009) and strip mining the air of its carbon so as to stay alive. 4,000 trillion kilowatts of energy reach the top of the atmosphere as sunlight, but only a small fraction of one per cent of that figure is ever captured by the pools of chlorophyll that are plants. That is still enough to turn hundreds of millions of tonnes of carbon dioxide into food and living tissue. In turn, this photosynthetic machinery regulates the planet, for example by adding all manner of material to the atmosphere that becomes the basis of aerosols. So when it is disturbed en masse – as humanity is now doing through forest clearance, for example – it produces all manner of wayward effects about which we often know very little and can influence even less.

Equally, plants have been revealed as active agents in the world. They can see, not in the same way as humans but not as simple cellular ciphers either. They detect light. They translate its varied visual signals into physiologically recognizable instructions. Plants smell too. They sense their own odours and those of neighbouring plants. They even warn each other of imminent insect attacks. Many plants perceive tactile sensation. They almost certainly react to sounds. They know where they are. They even remember certain things like past infections and climatic conditions (Chamovitz, 2012). So the impact of the Anthropocene on plants is many and varied and cannot be reduced to just one-way human impacts. Plants react back.

Finally, there is flesh. Animals are an immensely important element of the biosphere, a 'wildlife' we cohabit with in innumerable ways (Human Animal Research Network Editorial Collective, 2015; Lorimer, 2015). They are crucial to the earth's ability to maintain good running. Consider the total mass weight of living things on the planet. It is estimated to be in the order of 1.7 trillion tonnes, excluding bacteria. The overwhelming majority of this quantity is plant life – probably about 99 per cent.[2] The total human mass is at least about 350 million tonnes. Cows add in another 520 million tonnes. There are about 4200 million tonnes of fish and 2700 million tonnes of ants. Then bacteria weigh in at nearly the same as all other living things put together, at around 1.3 trillion tonnes[3] (D'Efillipo and Ball, 2013). But these brute numbers underplay animals' influence. For example, the humble nematode worm so beloved of scientists forms a film over the earth that makes it a decipherable entity. The tapeworm and a host of other parasites form an almost unimaginably rich layer of life. And this is to ignore those simple replicants, the viruses: studies have shown that 200 litres of seawater contain over 5,000 different types of virus, that there are more than a thousand viral species in a human stool and possibly a million different viruses per kilogram of marine sediment. In other words, 'take away humans and the present world will...function quite happily as it did two hundred thousand years ago. Take away worms and insects, and things would start seriously to fall apart. Take away bacteria...and the viruses and the world would die' (Zalasiewicz, 2009, p. 192).

Each of these different components of change mixes to differing degrees according to ecological imperatives that vary across the earth's surface. Ecologies change all the time, of course. Genetic soups are churned, sometimes (probably most times) creating more biodiversity. But currently these ecologies are changing at breakneck speed, colliding, miscegenating, collapsing or reforming as short-lived bastard hybrids. Perhaps the major sign of the rate of change is the annihilation of species. Humans are producing a mass extinction on the same scale as the catastrophic extinctions caused by asteroid impacts as they wipe out species directly or simply leave them marooned and so condemned to fade away. Human beings began erasing species, mainly megafauna, in the late Pleistocene, but now the pace has speeded up and encompasses all kinds of animals. 'It is estimated that one-third of all reef-building corals, a third of all freshwater mollusks, a third of sharks and rays, a quarter of all mammals, a fifth of all reptiles, and a sixth of all birds are headed toward oblivion' (Kolbert, 2014, p. 17). Extinction can come quickly. For example, the European invasion of the

USA produced a frightening ecological toll. Take the well-known case of the passenger pigeon. At one time the passenger pigeon was so abundant – one estimate is five billion birds – that flocks of pigeons would blot out the sun as they passed by, sometimes for hours at a time, and their short-lived nesting sites consisted of millions of birds distributed over as much as thirty square miles. From flocks more like battlefronts and colonies resembling cities to a lone individual. By September 1914 the last passenger pigeon had passed away in a Cincinnati zoo. Mass slaughter of a third of the biomass of all species of North American birds – twenty million passenger pigeons on average each year for a century – the loss of forest habitat, and a peculiar susceptibility based on a lifestyle reliant on very large numbers and a good half of a continent to roam over, reduced the passenger pigeon to an environmental will of the wisp and then to naught, taking numbers of species of dependent beetle and lice with them (Fuller, 2014; Greenberg, 2014). There have been many more such extinctions and extirpations, each and every one of them a tragedy of sorts. But it is too late now to shift their beginning. Equally, extinction can happen more slowly, through the genetic introgression fostered by movement.[4]

The other major sign of change is movement. Things move around in the Anthropocene to a greatly heightened degree, whether we are talking about minerals, atmospheres, plants or animals. So far as plants and animals are concerned, what is happening currently has been likened to a 'new Pangaea' (Kolbert, 2014). The old Pangaea was a supercontinent – all of our present continents merged together – which existed three hundred million years ago and which slowly broke apart, causing a divergence among species as they were split off one from another. Even with the phenomenon of long-distance dispersal, no species could move very far or very quickly, causing a degree of stability. Now species no longer need to move under their own power. It is as though Pangaea has been reformed: 'humans are running geologic history backward and at high speed' (Kolbert, 2014).

Of course, plants and animals move and then mix in new combinations all the time. In a time of climate change as species move into new domains, this may hardly be news. But summarizing recent scientific research, de Queiroz (2014) argues that epic journeys by plants and animals – so-called long-distance dispersal – have always been a norm of life and a key driver in evolution: plant seeds were carried in the plumage of ocean-going birds, frogs and mammals as large as monkeys were cast this way and that by driftwood and icebergs, tiny spiders drifted hither and thither on storm winds, and so on. These journeys may have been flukes but their consequences were not. But all that said, it is clear that human beings have redistributed a large part of the earth's flora and fauna, sometimes gradually, sometimes through ecological blitzkriegs. They have reassembled large parts of the biosphere so that what is native and what is not has become a loaded question, often linked to all kinds of strange variants on nationalism (Thompson, 2014). But, whatever the case, the photosynthetic machines we call plants have regularly swapped countries and continents. Take the case of Britain. Probably about 12,500 species of plants have been introduced into Britain through history, although only about two hundred count as fully established. Britain only had 35 native tree species a few thousand years ago, but many hundreds of others have now been added to the roster. So-called invasive species have become a major modern preoccupation, although only some of them have proved to be as ecologically disastrous as they are often painted (somewhere between 11 and 39 introduced plants currently count as pests in Britain) (Thompson, 2014). Indeed, as the British tree example shows, many introduced plants have increased biodiversity in positive ways. In cities, in particular, most species have been introduced. (Indeed, it is possible to argue that in cities even native plant species are exotic in the sense that they have colonized an artificial environment.)

Animals have been even more spatially promiscuous. Take the humble rat. The rat has piggybacked with human beings wherever they have journeyed on the earth's surface. Indeed, so numerous and well adapted to almost any conditions are these fellow travellers that they might well claim to be the main beneficiaries of human evolution (Zalasiewicz, 2009). The Pacific rat (*rattus exulans*) has travelled all around the Pacific, but its travels have been as nothing compared with the Norway rat (*rattus norvegicus*), actually from China originally, which has become common almost everywhere. Or take that living fossil and geographical adventurer, the ubiquitous cockroach. The average New Yorker is most likely to encounter the German cockroach, which probably originated in Southeast Asia, while the 'American' cockroach is actually a native of Africa. Rats and cockroaches – these are the main winners in the competition to colonize cities because they are so well adapted to adaptation. There are other examples too: mice, foxes, feral cats, deer, bears, camels (in Australia), houseflies, bedbugs and lice, even the humble snail. And that is before we light upon the case of domesticated dogs and cats. On one estimate, there are an estimated one billion dogs in the world and, like cats, they are an integral part of what cities are, companions in leisure and in misery, at least when they are not feral.

Of course, an extraordinary range of animals has been, for large swathes of history, the main means by which human beings have moved from place to place (Sturgis, 2015). This fact brings us neatly to that subset of animals known as human beings. Human movement has been a constant of history with consequent results such as genetic mixing. As human population sizes have increased and more and more mixing has taken place, so favourable mutations have been generated on an increasing scale. Even in the Bronze Age populations of less than sixty million were creating favourable mutations every four hundred years (Cochran and Harpending, 2009). The rise of agriculture forced more mutations to occur against a background of more and more population movement. It is worth noting that through history there has been a link between the mass movement of human beings – hastened by the increasing density of infrastructure, which allows that movement to take place more and more easily – and genetic mutation. If migration has been a constant condition of human history, it has picked up in pace and volume since the nineteenth century as movement has become easier and less hazardous. Each itinerant community arrives with its own genetic inheritance and spreads favourable mutations, as they mix in larger and larger cities in ways that are only starting to become clear.

To summarize, in the Anthropocene, as far as plants and animals are concerned, movement has become a natural state, hastened by infrastructure – what's under the hood, so to speak – which has become more and more adept at moving things around the second Pangaea.

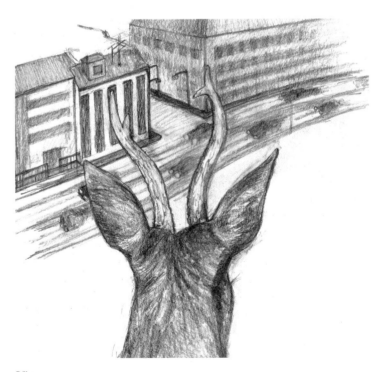

View

The Background Becomes Foreground

A good part of the reason for this motile state of affairs is the unremarked and mainly urban landscape that we pass every day which forms a second nature: power lines, concrete pavements and tarmac roads, street lights, manholes, traffic signals, mobile telephone towers, endless doors and windows, signs regulating movement – all the paraphernalia of city streets and industrial landscapes, in other words (Hayes, 2005). For many of us, this is what place is, not Heidegger's hut in Todtnauberg thrumming with the righteous glow of authenticity – a set of artificial networks with no real end point or finish line through which and on which we pass and are passed. These networks have produced a part of the planet that is ever in motion. The world is threaded with roads and cables, undergirded by pipes and tunnels and culverts, saturated by wireless signals, loaded down with all kinds of built infrastructure, and heated up by all manner of energy sources. It is criss-crossed by airline routes, lit up by innumerable street and other lights, and shaken by all manner of artificial sounds. And this infrastructure is composed of actual, physical 'stuff' that cannot be reduced to a discursive difference. As Bryant (2014, p. 5) puts it:

> Whether or not a commercial district grows as a function of the amount of energy available to that zone from the power plant is not a signifying or cultural difference. Whether or not people begin to die or move away as a result of pollution produced by garbage, coal-burning power plants and industrial waste is not a signifying difference. Whether or not people vote you out of office because they're angry about traffic congestion is not the result of a signifier. To be sure, there are social relations here insofar as it is people that produce all these things and people that are flocking into the city, moving away, or voting you out of office, but the point is that the form the city takes is not, in these instances, the result of a signifier,

a text, a belief or a narrative alone. It is the result of real properties of roads, power lines, pollution, and so on.

Infrastructure, in other words, consists of all of those objects that allow human beings, cars and trucks and boats and planes, water, sewage and other waste, oil, electricity, radio signals, information, and the like to flow from one place to another, to become mobile, to circulate. Mainly they consist of continuous conduits of one form or another but, increasingly, as wireless has become more common, these conduits have broadened out into signals transmitted from and received by masts, although the principle remains much the same. And this infrastructure is concentrated in cities because:

> cities require flows of energy and matter in order to maintain their organization and resist entropy. Cities, of course, require stone, brick, wood, plastics, metals and a variety of other materials out of which to build and maintain infrastructure. However, cities also require flows of energy to persist across time. They require wood, coal, electricity, the power of water and wind to heat homes, run transportation, and sustain various technologies. Yet they also require caloric energy. People must eat. (Bryant, 2014, p. 101)

The point is that the earth's surface has become a hundreds of kilometres high and at least four kilometre low anthropic stratum which is a bit like a Swiss cheese in its make-up, a stratum through which pipes and cables crawl, under which tunnels and boreholes and mineshafts bore down into the earth, on which all kinds of reservoirs and power sources hold sway and over which aeroplanes and satellites and wireless signals fly back and forth like Hermes, and nearly all of this activity is connected to the demands of cities.

This stratum may be thicker or thinner, but that it is remorselessly increasing in density is not in doubt. At the last G20 summit, for example, world leaders pledged to invest some sixty trillion dollars into new infrastructure by 2030. The International Energy Agency has estimated that, between 2015 and the middle of the century, more than fifteen million miles of new paved roads will be built worldwide (Nijhuis, 2015). Since 2007, China has carpeted its territory with nearly 20,000 kilometres of high-speed railways and wireless. In turn, the effects on the environment of infrastructure construction have often been drastic. Roads fragment habitats with clear effects on species loss. In one study, it was found that fragmented habitats lose an average of half of their plant and animal species within twenty years, and that some continue to lose species for thirty years or more.

So generic is all of this physical infrastructure that we take it for granted, at least until it goes wrong – think of the burst water main or the power cable brought down by an ice storm, or the missed delivery. Or think of much greater breakdowns of the kind occasioned by warfare; or by events like earthquakes or tsunamis or volcanic eruptions.[5] Equally, we forget that infrastructure has its own history: in effect, it is the history of a certain set of decisions made in the past about how to move things about, often based on military logistical principles, which have become a closed loop which is able to conceal its essentially political nature. To begin with, infrastructure is the history of changing the urban environment we live in. There are many examples of how infrastructure has performed in this regard, from heating to air conditioning (Basile, 2014), from piped water supply to piped music. But take the case of artificial lighting. Night-time is no longer another country, dark and forbidding. Thanks to reliable and constant artificial illumination produced by large industrial power networks, the 'sphere', to use Peter Sloterdijk's term, that we inhabit has expanded its orbit. Fingers of light stretch everywhere. The process began in Britain, which became a gaslight society when the first public street, Pall Mall in London, was lit with gas in 1807. Electric lighting arrived in 1878 but did not find its way into homes on a large scale until after the First World War. Artificial light has now spread all over the world, producing new apprehensions of how and what can be seen (Otter, 2008). But we should not overestimate this process of enlightenment: for many people in the world the dark is still dark. For example, in India in 2012, the largest electrical blackout in human history left 600 million people without power and therefore light. But discussing the blackout, Drèze and Sen (2013, p. 9) wryly noted that the media had neglected an important fact. 'Two hundred million of those 600 million people never had any power at all.'

Then, it is the history of how we are able to move about. This time, take the case of the humble lift upon which tall buildings rely for sustenance. Although records of lift design date back to Roman times, lifts (or 'ascending rooms') were first commonly used in the nineteenth century when hydraulic, steam and electric power were all used as sources of lift. In 1852, Elisha Otis introduced the first safety lift, which prevented the cab from falling if the cable suspending it broke, and in 1857 the first such passenger lift was installed in a building which still stands in the SoHo neighbourhood of Manhattan. The first office building to have passenger lifts, the Equitable Life Building, was completed, again in New York City, in 1870, and prefigured the growth of the late nineteenth-century commercial 'skyscraper' (a term first used then) and the consequent transformation of the skyline of many cities. The adoption of lifts had many consequences, apart from creating recognizable 'downtowns'. For example, before the use of lifts, most residential buildings were limited in height to about seven storeys. The wealthy lived on the lower floors, while the poorer residents lived on the higher floors, and were thus required to climb many flights of stairs. As exemplified by the modern penthouse, the lift reversed this stratification (Bernard, 2014). Now, as buildings have become ever taller (with a one-kilometre-high tower planned in Saudi Arabia), so lifts have become increasingly complex. Of course, they need to be faster (with speeds of up to eighteen metres per second) but they also need to include sky lobbies where passengers can change lifts to reach higher floors, and means of increasing capacity like double-decker lifts or multiple cabins in the same lift shaft.[6] The verticality of the city, rising not only far up into the air, but also digging deep into the ground, has yet to be properly grasped as a constitutive background (Graham, 2016).

Then, it is the history of how we move things around, quite literally. Take the case of maritime trade, a global infrastructure that has existed for many millennia. Europe, for example, has been a trading zone since at least 9000 BCE. But instead of amber, soapstone and shells brought overland or by sea and made into necklaces, bangles and the like (Cunliffe, 2011), our very bodies are now maps of global trade. Shirts, T-shirts and blouses from Thailand and China, coats from Malaysia, spectacles and contact lenses from Germany, watches from Switzerland, shoes from the United States: each of us is a lesson in exchange, a world in miniature. And we live in places chockful of stuff that has transited from other places by sea and still contains those places' echoes. Maritime trade depends upon a forest of rules and regulations which range from the international law of the sea to the humblest health and safety inspections and regulations, which includes the 100,000 freighters on the seas at any one time carrying nearly everything we eat, wear and work crewed by an itinerant population numbering in the hundreds of thousands (George, 2013) and which also includes the ports, full of specialized equipment ready to load and unload the containers which are the basic grammar of maritime trade (Levinson, 2006). And infrastructure has all kinds of other effects too. Most particularly, in allowing people to move, it allows all kinds of communities to spread out across the world. So there is the serried history of the diasporas that have arisen out of population movement, striking in their extent. In large part, the history of countries like Australia and the USA is the history of wave upon wave of diasporic communities. Migration has been a constant condition of human history, but it has picked up in pace and volume since the nineteenth century as movement has become easier and less hazardous. All kinds of discontinuous diasporic spaces have been created, many based on simple economic incentive but some the result of concerted state and state-related action like ethnic cleansing (Osterhammel, 2014). But movement is also born out of other imperatives too – like tourism, religious observance (consider the hajj) and all manner of other motives.

So ubiquitous is infrastructure like lighting – New York has over 250,000 street lights which are gradually being replaced with LED bulbs – and lifts – New York has at least 64,000, according to the city's buildings department – that this infrastructure has become an accepted feature of the landscape. In turn, it has spawned sites which can themselves be counted as infrastructure: ports, airports, railway stations, service stations have all become stock scenes of human conduct, places where we expect certain classes of movement drama to play out – meetings and farewells, temporary sojourns where it is possible to eat or refuel, places to gather and disperse, uneasy encounters and serendipitous meetings – against a background which is made as predictable as it can be, from the identical architecture to the uniforms. Augé (2009) once called them 'nonplaces', but as a description that is very far off the mark. Rather, they are 'by-places' which depend on the by-products of the journeys of people and things for their existence.

Then how we experience urban space begins to be mediated by infrastructure in ways that strike at the heart of our experience, as we began to argue in the preceding chapter. Take the case of sound. In the past, the sound-scapes of cities left room for sounds emanating from natural sources. Church bells might produce a periodic cacophony, especially in larger towns and cities, the noise of horse-drawn traffic might create a low roar at certain times of the day, and various shouts and bursts of music interspersed the daily round. But there were also periods of quiet and many acoustic spaces in which sound still consisted of the wind and birdsong (Glennie and Thrift, 2009). Now, things are very different. Places where the only sound is natural sound are few and far between – in Britain, you have to go far into a remote Northumbrian bog to find the quietest place. Cities are chockful of noises which form their own acoustic ecology, noises which become their own associative landscapes intensifying and fading as we move around – from the distant sound of aircraft overhead through the hum and honking of traffic to snatches of music and conversation, each with their own arcs (Gandy and Nilsen, 2014). Meanwhile, the world has become so beset by noise that great tits are forced to sing faster and higher in

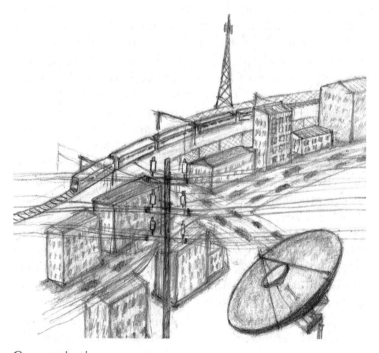

Communication

the urban din, and robins have taken to singing at night when it is quieter. Shipping noise disturbs the breeding of whales and dolphins: whales are having to sing louder and louder – and in some cases have given up entirely. (But there are also radio quiet zones around a few large radio telescopes to prevent interference from radio waves.) And the main reason why we can't get away from all this noise is – infrastructure.

Streams of (Un)consciousness

Cities are, of course, the places where infrastructure is thickest, and its experience most pressing, as the example of sound demonstrates. But they are also the places where new kinds of infrastructure have been invented and applied most fully – from roads and wheels (Bulliet, 2016) to wireless masts and phones. Most particularly, physical infrastructure has been supplemented by a new wave of infrastructure arising out of microcomputational sensing and data-gathering capabilities and sponsored by the so-called security-entertainment complex which acts both at a remove from conventional physical infrastructure and as one of the main items carried on that infrastructure. If physical infrastructure was second nature, this new wave of infrastructure is best thought of as a *third nature* based on the mass transportation of culture around the world at speeds which would once have been thought impossible. This is the history of the rise of a different kind of flow infrastructure.

This third nature has its origins in cities in the rise of a print culture of indexical mediation, which, in turn, led to the rise of counting and coveting and reporting, and transcribing in bureaucracies. In turn, this bureaucratic imperative led to further infrastructural innovations and, most notably, the documentary tradition of files, indexes and the various paraphernalia surrounding them, all brought together in specialized spaces intended to focus and routinize (Vismann, 2008). Equally, it led to all manner of means of identification, from spatial locations like addresses (Tantner, 2015) to passes allowing access to particular spaces like passports. It also led to planning using maps, diagrams and, latterly, equations. In other words, it became increasingly easy to produce an exterior memory that could then be reworked.

Working alongside this semiotic infrastructure set up to manipulate signs of life in a classic disciplinary manner was, of course, money in its various forms, another kind of abstraction which relied on both bureaucratic infrastructure and the rise, especially, of bookkeeping. And, finally, since the eighteenth century in particular, large corporations grew in scale and displayed an increasing bias to diagrammatic/algorithmic thinking based in procedures, plans and quantitative indicators, all set down on paper, and, latterly, liberal amounts of management thinking intended to slot human beings into the right place in a corporation.

However, in the past fifty years another level of abstraction which can itself be legitimately counted as a form of infrastructure has become recognizable as a result of large-scale changes in information and communications infrastructures pushed by developments in security and entertainment which have allowed the machinism of infrastructure to be extended into many other aspects of life which were formerly passed by. All manner of new semiotic motors have come into existence which bypass representation and consciousness but can be counted as real presences in the world with important and sometimes devastating effects (Lazzarato, 2014). They operate outside of our direct perception but in ways that can significantly affect our activity in all manner of ways. In other words, as Hansen (2015, p. 23) and others have argued, they denote a new kind of experience: 'experience simply is not what it used to be'.

Take money again with all of its algorithms and protocols and equations and second-order derivatives. It has sprouted all manner of second-order instruments which can only exist because of this infrastructure: stock market indices, options and derivatives and the like, based on an infrastructure that depends not only on physical infrastructure like millions of miles of cable or server farms but also on software algorithms, datasets and statistics, equations and accountancy conventions (Esposito, 2012). And, recently, money has become an even more pervasive infrastructure because of the rise of new kinds of financial technology and especially payment systems that are, in effect, enormous automated ledgers. These systems are often called 'rails' in obeisance to their infrastructural qualities.

Or take science that can only exist nowadays because of computation and equations that link the atomic and the chemical, the biological and the cosmic. Or take mass consumption that is reliant on a series of innovations that have allowed the mass personalization of consumers, most especially based around the integration of big data, advertising and the crafting of relationships. Or take mass media stratagems where computation and instantaneous communication allow an impersonal and preconscious rendition of the personal to take hold through temporary operative stabilities, listings which do not originate in the individual subject – but are designed to act as though they do (Fuller and Goffey, 2012). Or take government, which increasingly relies on the differential management of plural publics as part of a security state held together by data.

These machines do not act on consciousness as such but rather impact directly on the affective level as 'the continuous variation and force of existing and potential action' (Guattari, 2014), made concrete by asignifying elements pulsing directly through the body like rhythm, temporal cues, spatial formats, the variation and intensity of luminosity and colour, and sexuality. T'was always thus, one might say. But access to this realm is now much more easily brokered and worked upon, presentified and intensified if you like (Thrift, 2007). In each case, signs and things engage each other outside representation: monetary signs act directly on production, computer languages make machines run and communicate with each other directly, and so on. And they do this before the event, before they show up as the concerns of consciousness (Thrift, 2007). The result is, as Hansen (2015, p. 25) points out:

> Consciousness takes on what, contrasted with its near-absolute privilege in the history of Western philosophy, cannot but appear to be a more humble role as a modulator of a sensory presencing that takes place outside its experiential purview.

In other words, another kind of impersonal personal infrastructure now exists in the world, a third nature made up of a set of machineries of individuation which is both plural and singular in character (Esposito, 2012): 'the higher-order, complexly embodied human operations have been fundamentally displaced in a world of microtemporal computational media' (Hansen, 2015, p. 26). This imperfect but still potent machinery bears many resemblances to physical infrastructure but the machinery consists of algorithmic systems of systems, circulating machinisms that accompany our daily lives. These machinisms both assist and undergird our ways of speaking, hearing, seeing, writing, feeling and thinking by providing an infrastructure of constant sociability, an infrastructure which creates a predictable set of bubbles of time and space through the assignment of all manner of structured recurrences. These recurrences are etched on our bodies and brains as expected nonrepresentational behaviours that are deterministic even as they grant what seems like a high degree of elasticity of choice. Such machinisms are not separate from or implanted into human life, but coextensive with it, not least because, like much of human life, they operate at the preverbal level as a built equivalent of punctuation rather like a comma which is both a stop and a tie.[7] These machinisms may assign subjective roles but they also include us in infrastructural assemblages which no longer distinguish between living and dead, human and non-human, subject and object, or words and things: 'there are as many living beings in the machine as there are machines in the living' (Deleuze and Guattari, 1983, p. 286). Individuals are literally cogs in a larger 'dividual' machine (Lazzarato, 2014). They are catchphrases in machines consisting of various hybrid animations/automatisms that add up to a process of flow in which intelligence and cognition, sensations and affects, and memory and desire are all lumped together in a diagrammatic, nonrepresentational way and manipulated through modelling and modulation such that nonperceptual potentiality becomes actuality. The essential public good is now a privatized hybridized 'us' which is being written into the world through screens of all kinds and, latterly, sensors and new computational 'metamaterials' which act as ecologies rather than simple technologies and produce an 'environmental subjectivity (Meek, 2014; Thrift, 2007, 2014). The result is that 'human experience is currently undergoing a fundamental transformation caused by the complex entanglement of humans within networks of media technologies that operate, predominantly, if not almost entirely, outside the scope of human modes of awareness' (Hansen, 2015, p. 5).

Such 'asignifying' signs are machinisms that function whether they necessarily mean something for a constituency or not in that they prescribe themselves as they describe themselves (Johnston, 2014). They are diagrams 'whose functions are operational, rather than representational' (Lazzarato, 2014, p. 86). Think punctuation marks again. Their main goal, in other words, is to reproduce a set number of operations by acting as partially discursive and partially nondiscursive entities but operating to the side of the language we ordinarily use, instead using cues which consist of sets of machinic instructions – like computer code. They produce multiple realities. Thus, as Lazzarato (2014, p. 92) argues in the case of financial trading, there is 'the reality of the "real" economy, the reality of forecasts about the economy, as well as the reality of share prices and the reality of expectations about these prices rising or falling'. Each of these multiple realities has its own indexes and data and diagnostics, its own evaluative software, and its own diagrams. Much of what counts as each form of reality is either outside explicit human control, consisting of machines communicating with machines, or nudges human thoughts and actions into certain well-defined tramlines through institutional-ized forms of technical imitation like measures of various kinds. Multiple decisions are being made, then, but they are often outside a conventionally human purview of con-sequential alternatives (Amoore, 2013).

Orientation

Back to the City

But what has all this to do with the city? Machinic ways of working like these might be thought of as a part of the creation of urban 'hyperobjects' (Morton, 2013), a term we will return to in due course. Cities are human presences but they are more than that, not least because not all of their activity can be made present to thought and because they consist of many intersecting modes of existence. We have created in cities something that has its own kind of causality but one that does not just coincide or correlate with us. In making this point, we obviously run squarely across the correlationist conceit that the world only exists within a narrow bandwidth – the human and what the human counts as the world. 'Meaning is only possible', according to this conceit, 'between a human mind and what it thinks, its "objects", flimsy and tenuous as they are' (Morton, 2013, p. 9). 'There is no thinking of reality without thinking of it' (Gratton, 2014, p. 6), in other words. But that conceit omits much of what exists – the world beyond how it appears to us – a 'what' that, in any case, continually impinges on the human, come what may, and which we can certainly speculate about. In other words, a part of the philosophical conversation has turned from *how* we know reality to *what* the stuff of reality might be (Gratton, 2014), given that it cannot be reduced to one set of primordial entities.

Whatever that 'what' is – and there are many arguments about this – it is not simply a human domain but nor is it simply 'other' and therefore able to be swept under the carpet. To put it another way, things can belong to the social without being socially constructed. Equally, there can be nonhuman social assemblages (like coral reefs). There is no rigid argument to be had in these circumstances: matter can shift about, can become something else, according to how it is aligned, and infrastructure is one of the chief ways of achieving this.

Cities are social assemblages but equally they exist as a nonhuman domain. How might we think about them as entities when they are seen in this light, to add to the account already begun in the preceding chapter? One way is through Morton's (2013) fruitful notion of cities as hyperobjects, a status they gain by dint of the properties they display, many of which are both in and outside human awareness, exerting a gravitational pull that we can't help but feel but cannot necessarily put into words. (Intuition, suggestion and fantasy are just three of the ways we attach meaning to these foreign objects (Berlant, 2011; Harman, 2012).) According to Morton, a number of properties are particularly germane in sketching the urban hyperobject. To begin with, cities are *viscous*; that is, it is impossible to get away from the field of concurrences they generate. Cities stick to us: like it or not, we are a part of them. Then they are *nonlocal* in the sense that everything existing in them has ties to other locations; they are the embodiment of action at a distance and, at the same time, hyperconnected so that they cannot easily be separated into distinct but interacting parts or into the general and the particular – everything overflows, everything is wrapped in something else, everything that exists always coexists. Again, they are *temporally discontinuous* with human lives. They consist not only of human-scale thoughts and practices but also of all manner of modes of sentience with their own timelines and modes of intervention in the world. None of them is necessarily consistent with the others but each of them is able to interfere with each other because their parts do not have to become a single whole: city never becomes City. Yet, at the same time, everyone is affected in some way by city: cities are also forms of regularity which impose a kind of order on this surging, vibrant crowd of becomings, as infrastructural meshes both emitting and capturing spacetimes. Finally, cities are configurational. The different combinations of integration and connectivity of the various links that go to make up cities produce differential effects which act as sublunary compasses, as 'space syntax' (Hillier, 1999).

We can think of a number of ways of invoking these knots of teeming activity. For example, cities can be thought of as *ontographs*, interobjective piles of beings brought into alignment via locative infrastructures like streets and pipes, an alignment on which causality has been inscribed but only very loosely: don't forget that cities also have cul-de-sacs, abandoned and derelict plots, roads to nowhere (Bogost, 2012). Or cities can be thought of as a spatially configured *multiverse* in which each universe bears the imprint of the others, is ontologically bound to its siblings, in other words, as a mix of mixes (Rubenstein, 2014). Or cities can be thought of as a meta-form like grids, which manifest both variety and evolution and are able to encompass both building and unbuilding (Higgins, 2009; Hommels, 2005). Whatever the case, in a city there is no simple presence or absence or foreground and background or natural and unnatural or withdrawn and sensual to be found: these concepts have evaporated as infrastructure moves things around and between cities. But there is a sense of nearness and intimacy, even if not a sense of belonging, which is brought about by alignments that may be regular and predictable but may equally flicker like an early silent movie, reach a standoff like two dogs fighting to a standstill or even come to rest like an exhausted migratory bird.

> Think of a city. A city contains all kinds of paths and streets that one might have no idea of on a day-to-day basis. Yet even more so, you could live in a city such as London for fifty years and never fully grasp it in its scintillating, oppressive, joyful London-ness. The streets and parks of London, the people who live there, the trucks that drive through its streets, constitute London but are not reducible to it. London is not a whole greater than the sum of its parts. Nor is London reducible to those parts. London can't be 'undermined' downward or upward. Likewise,

London isn't just an effect of my mind, a human construct
– think of the pigeons in Trafalgar Square. Nor is London
something that only exists when I walk through the Victo-
ria Line tunnel to the Tate Gallery at Pimlico Underground
Station, or when I think about London. London can't be
'overmined' into an after-effect of some (human) process
such as thinking or driving or essay writing. (Morton,
2013, p. 91)

But let's not get too romantic about these things. Cities
may leave all kinds of gaps and generate all manner of
unexpected revelations. But none of this is to suggest that
the systems of systems of third nature cannot provide
extraordinary levels of panoptic surveillance that seem to
act as a shroud around each and every event, tying the
possibility of possibilities into duelling knots. Take the
example of the way in which American cities corral young
male African Americans. As Goffman (2014) shows in her
controversial book on one of the poorer areas of Philadelphia, they can be caught up in a system of law enforce-
ment so punitive and panoptic that it is difficult to forge
anything except a life as a criminal. Multiple databases,
a squad car filled with information technology, blanket
policing and a blizzard of warrants produce outcomes
that are both implacable and almost always malign. It can
often seem as if these parts of cities are simply extensions
of prisons, part of a new Jim Crow (Alexander, 2012).

Their very complexity, however, also makes it hard
to keep these systems of systems functioning like this in
logistical lockstep for concerted periods of time. Not that
it hasn't been tried. Think only of some of the ways in
which socialist planning manifested itself in cities by locating representatives of the state on every city block or the
various means of contemporary urban surveillance from
urban passports through ubiquitous cameras to drones.
Think only of the way in which halting attempts to build
systems that could cope with emergency produced a patchwork of systems that could manage states of emergency,
systems that have gradually migrated into government as

usual (Collier and Lakoff, 2015). Or think only of China's attempts to construct a new Great Wall, a Golden Shield or Great Firewall, within which information can be strictly controlled. But each of these systems, however tightly they are drawn, has cracks, moments of breakdown or confusion, bypasses, interpretative overloads, jagged edges, missing pieces and simple errors which can add up to a new and enticing opportunity for someone. In other words, even systems of systems find it difficult to dry out the world, much as they might try to do so. There will always be room for politics – but what kinds of politics will continue to be an open question. After all, that question is itself political.

Furthermore, it is now overlaid by an Anthropocene whose effects are far-reaching. The term has been described as primarily 'a politically savvy way of presenting to nonscientists the sheer magnitude of biophysical change' (Castree, 2014, p. 233). But this is to miss the point. The Anthropocene does far more than this. It 'questions the seeming self-evidence or coherence of... basic conceptions' (Clark, 2015, p. 20) like the human, the social and the cultural. It puts so much stress on the standard categories of Western thinking that it shatters them. Instead it ushers in a perspectivist world in which all manner of becomings and relations jostle against each other in no particular order of eminence and prevail over being and substance. A people receptive to any shape and able to believe in everything. In particular, the idea of a system of beliefs with its implications of sovereignty and rule can be replaced with something more malleable, an ontology 'consisting of essential ontological incompleteness – the incompleteness of sociality and in general of humanity' (Viveiros de Castro, 2011, p. 47), not least because humanity radically expands its definition of human so that others are a solution and not, as they have been in so much Western thinking, a problem.

Cities illustrate something else too. They are both an assertion of human dominion and a challenge to it. Many writers on economic development and growth simply assume that the expansion of a human-dominant world is a fact of life. But the Anthropocene lays down a challenge to this account. It does so in several ways. First, it points to the fact that there must be an end point to this process on a planet with finite resources. Perhaps human dominion is an evolutionary dead end. Second, it challenges us to think of new models of the human. For example, we might think of humanity as a detrivorous species, one that, similarly to earthworms or slugs, digs up dead material and releases it as energy into the environmental system and, as a result, is caught in a 'bloom and crash cycle' because it lacks biogeochemical circularity. Or, we might think of it as a hive species, intent on building a mammalian of insect eusociality by other means than those found among orders like hymenoptera (ants, bees and wasps). Again, we might think of it as a species that is so plastic that the environmental spheres it etches, the self-realizing forms that Sloterdijk (2011) calls 'animated interiorities', are different variants of adulthood. Third, they highlight Isabelle Stengers' issue of inheritance: who and what is it we want to inherit from in a time when agency itself is changing, when who and what have become ever more malleable? Cities are both the object and the subject of this question, not least because they both concentrate space and time through the intricate processual couplings that have become possible through infrastructure (Hamilton, Bonneuil and Gemenne, 2015). And, finally, the obvious but still neglected empirical point: cities are always and everywhere orchestrated by human *and* nonhuman means. They are a series of knots which rely on various kinds of attunement in which infrastructure is a vital thread. They are always and everywhere live mappings, constantly constructing patchy and incomplete but still productive propositions out of often unintentional assemblages and blurring the boundaries between ordinary and extraordinary as they do so (Tsing, 2015).

Crossroads

– 3 –

How Cities Think

Keiko was not one of our kind but nonetheless he was still
one of us.
Veterinary chaplain speaking at the funeral of Keiko, a
killer whale, 2003, cited in Berreby, 2006

Beware that, when fighting monsters, you yourself do not
become a monster...for when you gaze long into the
abyss. The abyss gazes also into you.
Nietzsche

A thousand years to climb from ghosts and magic to
technology; a day and a half from technology back up to
ghosts and magic.
Watts, 2014, p. 148

So how do cities declare themselves? How do they manifest? How do they listen? How do they craft responses that
are efficacious? What counts as the effort of doing this? To
answer questions like these, we need, above all, to avoid
reductionist accounts of the city while realizing that the
city forms a web which travels through us and as us but
which also takes in many other kinds of entities as it edges

forward, The question of urban form becomes more than incidental but it is mixed in with a fertile but also challenging politics of cognition, of what thinks where and in what registers. As Clark (2015, p. 21) notes:

> The Anthropocene names a newly recognized context that entails a chastening recognition of the limits of cultural representation as a force in human affairs, as compared to the numerous economic, meteorological,[1] geographical and microbiological factors as well as scale effects, such as the law of large numbers.

So, to begin with, as we argued in Chapter 1, we need to ask what is 'is' in an urban setting, and simultaneously what counts as 'human' in that setting, and how cities complicate and sometimes completely unravel this distinction.

It should be clear by now that we are bending towards a very different notion of human based on the fundamentally *associative* ability of cities to mix and match through a pidgin of subjects and objects moderated by urban form. But that does not mean that we want to lose the notion of the human entirely. Rather, we want to unpeel a different sense of human – 'Homo civitatis' – based in the sensorium that the city now provides which is felt but in an expanded body which plays with Deleuze's classical question: what can a body do? This might appear to be a rather chilly view of the human, bereft of many of the special romances we have told ourselves about ourselves about 'modernity', each with its own narratives, characterizations and moral payoffs (Kenny, 2014), in favour of tangled threads of threads with no easy beginnings or endings, but, as the saying goes, that's life.

Equally, we want to inject an element of wonder back into how we go on. The way the world turns up should be a matter of wonder. Think of the myriad interactions that mean things appear on the doorstep or in supermarkets, at least in certain parts of the world. Or the fact that the lights stay on and fresh water flows through taps. Or the way that we are able to travel from a to b without too much hassle. It is almost impossible to conjure up the existential complexity – and the corresponding fragility – of the bedrock of civilization that is infrastructure. Yet we consistently filter wonder out of how we regard the world as it goes on going. With all those interactions, each with the possibility of a swerve, we remain unimpressed. We are not amazed. We are not astonished. And, as Sloterdijk (2015) points out, nowhere is more of a wonder-free zone than the social sciences. Millions, nay billions, of people are bound together in 'societies' by infrastructure and all that it compels in ways that can only be described as extraordinary. Yet as people and all manner of other entities hurtle ahead, social scientists often seem to do their best to strip them of contemplation of the rails that they run along, arranging them as though they are a simple board game rather than a humming force propelled by their own inventions. The wonder is lost. It has to lie down and beg for attention.

If urbanicity, Anthropocene and infrastructure demand that we think about the 'human' in a broader way, as a composite of technical and earthly powers, and in a narrower way, as a set of colliding planes of subjection which do not neatly add up to an 'individual', then how can we signal human action in ways which are inventive but do not just randomly gather facts from the skip at the end of the road? How can we think not of a person but of a climate, to paraphrase Auden on Freud? And more broadly, what happens when that climate changes as infrastructure becomes more and more pervasive? That requires thinking about infrastructure differently. It is not dull and inert. It is lively.

This chapter addresses these questions by marrying what is left of the subject with the broader infrastructural networks that characterize modern cities, as outlined in the last two chapters. Thus the first part of the chapter, a prelude to a more general investigation of *Homo civitatis*, is concerned with a description of the human as a spatial product that takes into account modern discoveries about what and what doesn't separate the human from other species. The second part of the chapter then addresses what happens when the human is broken apart and put back together in cities, surrounded by a mantle of objects that stretch and integrate the human into urban space. The third part of the chapter broadens out still further. What happens when cities themselves think? How does the human relate and thrive within a complex of relations, which is by definition extra-human? We point to six different ways in which these questions need to be explored in order to produce practical solutions. Finally, the concluding part of the chapter suggests that capturing this world requires a careful study of how the urban world gains more and more dimensionality and shifts its spectrum. Here various fantastical literary forms provide inspiration in that they cast cities as transcending the border of what is counted as efficacious or even real and provide guides to how we might think about how cities might be understood in different ways which move away from anthropocentrism towards other kinds of thought which displace the human, or at least stock accounts of what it is to be human.

What seems certain is that Homo civitatis is a very different animal from what we have often thought to be the human rootstock. It is bound to an environment which increasingly attempts to make the human feel as though the world is at its beck and call – through money and consumption, personalized mass media like the internet, and all manner of – while making sure through security apparatuses, personalized mass media, and the like – that it is actually the human that is at the city's beck and call. Yet the city is still set within a world of ruptures between the world and humans that cannot be gainsaid and especially an assumption that resources will continue to be forthcoming on a planet that is being drained of its goodness. Perhaps, as Serres (2014) argues, there is now a gap between this new reality and the organizations generally created at a time when humanity lived very differently. Whatever the case, one of the key items on the agenda of change will be infrastructure. Infrastructure will need to become a different kind of beast. And so, accordingly, will a stumbling humanity (Gray, 2015).

Messenger

The Accidental Species

'Humanity' is, it has to be said, a moveable feast. Gee (2014) shows that the messy evolutionary outcome we choose to call a baseline, 'human', is only one possibility out of many, one which flatters our prejudices to be sure, but one that owes more to chance than to any special estate in which an inevitable arc of human exceptionalism leads to well-deserved supremacy over the earth – especially when the evolutionary record shows that, for example, the loss of functions is as pervasive in evolution as gain and that several hominins once inhabited the earth in parallel (so that even now it is by no means clear why *Homo sapiens* won out).

Gee starts his anti-culmination account with the peculiar posture of bipedality, which he shows could just as well have arisen entirely by accident, as a by-product of something like sexual selection and certainly not as a causal process with an avowed effect in mind such as freeing up the hands to use tools or to provide better care for offspring, or what have you. He then moves on to other supposedly unique attributes: to technology – many animals (apes, birds, even octopuses), it is now known, make and use tools and produce structures outside the body like honeycombs, termite nests and anthills, and coral reefs – to large brain size or volume – other animals have larger brain size or volume – to language – special in its mode of delivery perhaps but not in its function of communication – and, finally, sentience – other animals are self-aware too. For example, 'not only can crows think things through, they are capable of thinking through what they are thinking through. And they are also capable of thinking through what other crows are thinking through' (Gee, 2014, p. 136). In each case, Gee shows systematically that each of the attributes regarded as supposedly uniquely human are alive and well and living through much of the animal world and they are the outcome of a process of evolution which is not unique to our species. It seems that there is no core human quality but rather different processes of humanization that vary with time. But if 'some species have communication systems, can predict what happens next, can solve certain social and physical problems, have traditions and perhaps even empathy' (Suddendorf, 2014, p. 14), there are four attributes which have clearly pushed our evolution in a particular direction. They are not so much exceptions as they are endowments that have proved multiplicative rather than additive. They have produced an enhanced evolutionary momentum by reworking volition.

One of these attributes – the most obvious – is sociality. We are built to be extraordinarily cooperative: our bodies ooze this affective-cognitive compulsion in the way that their anatomy has evolved. Thus there is the voice (mouth), which transmits information not only through linguistic content but also through pitch, rhythm and intensity. There is the face – by some estimates more data are transmitted through facial expression than what we say. There is gesture – body language is a vital organ of communication. And there is touch – the skin and especially the hand are both signalling systems and affective warrants. Each anatomical register contributes to a sense of connection that is also a *surface* in that it defines, in conjunction with available technology, how we are able to *reach* others and what our intuitions about the world can be (Derrida, 2005). That surface can be made up of words but equally of lines and colours, sounds and images.

Whatever the register, we have an urge to connect and to keep on connecting: cooperation is pivotal to our evolving cognitive capacity (Sterelny, 2014). 'Even two-year-old children outperform great apes on tasks of social learning, communication, and intention reading. Other animals may give alarm calls and food calls but otherwise do not show many signs of a drive to share their experience and knowledge with others' (Suddendorf, 2014, p. 219). In turn, that compelling urge to connect has led to the development of signs and words and expressions that allow us to read others' minds, share their experiences and produce collective solutions to problems. The urge to connect leads to other things as well, and of course most notably the need to shape the world so that it fits our conceptions of preconceptions, for example through acts of categorization that divide people into those who fit and those who don't (Berreby, 2006) and, most crucially, through the constant reshaping of the environment itself.

Then, and relatedly, we amplify that urge to connect through the vital medium of 'nested scenario building' or – to put it colloquially – stories. We seem to be susceptible to imagining ourselves and others as participants in the drama of our own lives, and this brings us to another attribute which may be at least relatively unique; that is, our ability to make fictions, to invent virtual worlds of kaleidoscopic variety. Stories include the lessons learned by others. They give examples of how to solve problems. They create the bonds between people that lead to dynamic feedback loops of polyvalent conception. We act as though these bonds are real and so they are. In many ways, the stories are the medium of humanity, a rush of words that constitute what we are rather than the other way around. The transmission is more important than the individual transmitters who, most of the time, simply pass things on like ants or bees, sure of what they know – which is very little.

Third, we are phenotypically plastic: our minds develop differently in different environments as we learn to forage in different ways. The brain is sufficiently plastic that we can talk about people who have encountered different environments having different neurogeographies. And this development continues because we have another related characteristic: we are neotonous. We retain juvenile traits into adulthood, partly because we grow at a very slow tempo and retain many foetal traits. The goal of adulthood is to develop what are often still considered childlike traits like knowing and learning, exploring, experimenting and wondering. We fail to grow up and we continue to learn and play and show curiosity into old age, traits that in other animals tend to be found predominantly in the young. We are adept at 'growing young', to use Montagu's (1983) famous phrase. But that also means that we have a pressing need for diversion. We need to fill time with activity, to poach from Pascal's *Pensées*.

But we should not let language and imagination automatically take on a sovereign role. So, last, the human is a machinic, hive entity. 'Twas always thus, one might argue. The conscious being entire unto itself, the 'ego tunnel' (Metzinger, 2010), is a human invention. But the dots can never actually be joined up. 'The cave of self is empty' (Metzinger, 2003, p. 633). There is no one there whose illusion the conscious self might be. That is not to say that it isn't easy to see how a subjectively experienced and reflexive identity of self and world can emerge, both as a unitary identity and transtemporally, given both the high degree of situated coherence of the body and the fact that self-representation is dependent upon a reasonably sharp boundary being maintained between self and world. But working out how this identity patch feels and knows itself takes time and is easily undone. Language is obviously the important means of self-inscription here, and its consequences overflow since 'the self-model is what built the functional bridge from individual cognition to social cognition, from first-person intelligence to the pooling of resources in a species' (Metzinger, 2003, p. 603). But it is more accurate to say that there is an outside world and an inner, unconscious mind, but we directly perceive neither of them. Rather, both our outward perceptions and our inward consciousness are a kind of interface, a membrane between the mind and the world. Everything that we experience is 'a virtual self in a virtual reality' (Metzinger, 2010). It is that membrane we need to concentrate on, a relationship between brain, body, and the entities of the 'external' world. What recent research shows is that it is very flexible. That does not mean that there are no neurophysical constraints, but it is also clear that it can be shaped by all manner of influences. Take the case of spatial perception. Map reading seems to be a considerable human ability. Even quite young children have an ability to place themselves on a map, partly because human beings seem to have some core geometric competences that are phylogenetically ancient (Huang and Spelke, 2014). But there are still remarkable cultural differences in how 'maps' are understood and apprehended which are part and parcel of more general differences in spatial apprehension (Levinson and Wilkins, 2006). What we mark as space, in other words, is a matter for the membrane which is certainly culturally shaped but also depends on all manner of other factors, from the kind of landscape in which spatial learning takes place to the degree of invariance of perception of forms.

The escape from a centred view of the self also makes it easier to understand contemporary processes of subjectivation. As we noted in the last chapter, these now rely on the mass production of individuality and localization for their potency (Lazzarato, 2014). Through many different conduits, as a matter of course, dividualled individuals are assembled which act in ways which are parodic but feel authentic. This is a new kind of cartographic 'existentialization' regime, a regime very different in nature from previous disciplinary and pastoral regimes. It has become easier to impose because of a general growth in knowledge of how to pre-programme affect, because information technology makes it possible to stick with each body twenty-four hours a day and continually reinitiate behaviours, because advances in visual and sound technology have allowed messaging to become more sophisticated, and generally because the enhanced power of editing and selection has enabled collective logics to become stickier and more at home in almost any situation. In this regime it becomes easier to map out and hold existential territories that in previous times were much less easy to control. As the various more or less consistent cartographic machines are deployed, so they generate subjective territories through the engineering of disposition and the very fact of acting into a situation. But because they act as predicates, they also continue to generate possibility and not just narrative orthodoxy.

Another way of putting this is that the brain is remarkably malleable and can link with and become a part of all kinds of things (Malabou, 2008). These couplings, in turn, require the acquisition of new powers or the capacity for new operations. Many of these couplings work through

the brain's mechanisms of largely nonconscious, endo-
genous self-regulation. They can, of course, be besieged
or destroyed, both by physical traumas of many kinds
which require the brain to build a new subjectivity, or by
cultural events which are sufficiently strong that they can
be equated with these neuro-traumas or, at least in theory,
by psychoanalytic and other therapeutic strategies which
can simulate trauma and build a new subjectivity (Johnston, 2014). In other words, the brain is characterized by
considerable plasticity and that plasticity allows it to make
all manner of unexpected and sometimes wayward links
that may give it quite different powers.

Finally, as the preceding chapter has made clear, the
human is identified as twisted into knots of things. Things
surround us. They cosset us. They threaten us. They become
us. There are, of course, many different kinds of things with
many different kinds of powers. And things come together
in many different combinations, producing, through this
process of everyday quilting, many new powers. In the
past, such a depiction of the world might have been taken
for naive realism, but, with the rise of speculative realism,
that is no longer the case. In turn, other consequences
arise. In particular, human exceptionalism is once again
revealed as a problematic state of affairs. For example,
the classic notion that humans (themselves things) make
artefacts in a hylomorphic manner, assembling them in
their mind and then imposing them on artefacts through
unidirectional agency, has been replaced by a much more
complex relationship in which the artefact negotiates with
the maker just as the maker negotiates with the artefact.
In turn, the world of things is revealed as consisting of a
complex system of entities with very different degrees of
potency and resonance, but one thing it is not is passive.
The world of things is more like a weather system, constantly shifting position, constantly mutating, constantly
exerting a pull. It is a series of swipes at life, stubs of
meaning, not a tidy narrative. It begins before it begins and
ends before it ends. To apprehend it, we need to 'learn to

speak in several voices' (Serres, 2012, p. 79) like a chorus able to draw on several sources and not just the human.

Events

Growing Young? The Demise of the Baseline Human

So we may have located the human as more or less an accident 'with no clear insight into what moves us to live as we do' (Gray, 2015, p. 137), and we may have diluted the human – broken it up and put it back together as so many reciprocating and strophic infrastructures producing

individuations rather than hard and fast subjects – and
we may have shown that the human occupies a world of
things which mould it as much as they are moulded by it,
but that does not, of course, mean that humanity does not
exist. Rather, it has taken on a new, less rigid, carapace
or, to return to previous language, membrane. Humanity
has extended its physical range through various internal
and external prostheses, moving its reach outside the body
through various means as different as and inwards through
means like. In the future, we can already be fairly certain
that: smart metabolic biomaterials and optogenetics will
make all surfaces into screens that can be interrogated, will
make 3D printing seem a primitive hold-out and will make
functional anatomy a consumer good; that digital menus
and barcodes will set computer programs and bacteria and
viruses free to roam, producing new meanings of print but
hopefully not in weaponized form; and that simulation
will become an everyday means of negotiation. The result
is that the human membrane has been technologized. But
the problem is that 'technology' is an inadequate description of the membrane. It does not sufficiently convey the
ecological third nature of what is taking place, as humans
become climates existing in an in-between as much as in
a separate envelope.

Indeed, part of the problem is that since the second half
of the twentieth century humanity exists too much, not just
as a seething mass of bodies seemingly intent on turning
the planet into a termites' nest, but as what Serres (2014)
calls a 'hominescence', a new ecological efflorescence of the
human based on a re-engineering of the various faculties
of the body (which are increasingly outsourced); the ubiq-
uity of transport and communication, and the increasing
density of global hyperobjects (like the internet, genomic
manipulation and nuclear power and, of course, climate
change) which we have produced but do not control. Most
particularly, this new humanity's main talent is its ability
to produce vast, mainly temporary, collectivities all set

within what Serres (2014, p. 6) calls a 'new city' which is both compressed and extensive.

> Invariant in its variations, it comprises and shuffles all cities through thousands of intercity webs, in which, for instance, the largest 'restaurant' in the world belongs to the most important American airline. France becomes a city with the TGV as its subway system and the freeways as its streets.

This new kind of city, with its genies and spirits, begins to resemble nothing so much as a kind of technological forest, chockful of selves only some of which will chime depending on the context (Kohn, 2013; Thrift, 2014). We will call this context an aperture in that it is the space through which meaning about what constitutes an 'I', a 'you', a 'we' or an 'it' is able to pass. This aperture is both a constraint and a resource. But what is certain is that it does not project human qualities everywhere: it reaches beyond the human, producing a new 'us' peopled by all manner of selves, only some of which are human. In turn, this stance produces a kind of transrealism – an ability to undermine a consensus reality but without providing any notion of an escape hatch into an overarching fantasy of control or a permanently on sense of the extraordinary. The goal is to produce a trans-entity pidgin which provides just enough communication to induce a productive level of discomfort which can lead on to new trans-entity forms and patterns, new generalities, abstractions and categories which allow different points of reference to be incarnated.

Technology will gradually revolutionize this process. Take that classic physiognomic icon, the face, and its qualities of faciality (Rodowick, 1997). We tend to see the world as a set of surfaces signifying qualitative states. It is often thought that the landscape that surrounds us can speak back in numerous ways, pressing on our flesh, making short work of our various vanities. But what if that landscape could now perceive our faces and read their contours for meaning, even beating a path through complexities like setting, light level and angle? That is no longer a pipe dream. Although facial recognition systems are still less than perfect, they can now begin to decode what is probably the main organ of emotional communication, which by some accounts transmits more data through facial expressions than through what we say – by making the face itself into a landscape, into a regional geography, which can be quantified, aggregated and leveraged (Khatchadourian, 2015). What if the close-up, formerly a property of cinema, became generalized?

> The organization of the face is undone in favour of its own material traits which become the building material... of an affect, or even a system of affects... this is the way in which the face participates in the nonorganic Life of things, pushing the face to its point of nudity and even inhumanity, as if every face enveloped an unknown and unexplored landscape.   (Smith, 1997, p. xxxii)

Technological effacement creates new surfaces in which 'I', 'you', 'we' and 'us' again become closer to the role of the ancient Greek chorus which was public and incantatory.

Import and export

Thinking Thinking Cities

So what is thinking in these transreal cities? We can start
with the Whiteheadian proclamation of the 'panpsychic'
immanence of thought everywhere: mentality is a basic
property of matter (Shaviro, 2014). If we take that thesis
to be correct (and the only alternative is eliminativism
which implies that being is devoid of thought), then cities
think as a matter of course. But we can also argue that
cities are increasingly able to think as wholes as well as
parts (Thrift, 2014), most especially through the expanded
use of informational technologies which have at least some
degree of feedback, response and adjustment built into
them, underlining Latour's point that the word 'matter'
is entirely too passive, singular and exterior to encompass what is going on in cities which is closer to a more
plural redefinition of matter as 'materials' (Latour, 2013).
Through a potent mixture of increased linkage between
things, combined with a mixture of sensors, screens and
other forms of display (like haptics) being conjured up
on any surface on demand as well as other 'smart' forms
of matter like smart dust and quantum dots enabled by
ubiquitous electronics and software, cities are increasingly
able to *think*, not in the same way as human beings, to
be sure – but in any case it is hardly likely that human
modes of thought cover all of the possibilities of thinking.
More likely, these cities manifest a form of noncorrelation-
ist thought, thought that is 'nonintentional, nonreflexive
and most often nonconscious, a kind of "autistic" thought
which is not correlative to being but immanently intrinsic
within it' (Shaviro, 2014, p. 12). This is 'noncorrelational
sentience' (Shaviro, 2014, p. 132) – nonreflexive, chiefly
nonconscious, nonphenomenological. But cities include
within their frame all kinds of entities that think in different ways, and not least human beings (who think in
all kinds of different ways too, of course), all kinds of
'scales and registers of life, both organic and inorganic'

(Manning, 2013, p. 226), that resonate together in all manner of dispositional ways. In cities, thought is therefore always open and pluralist.

In particular, cities come to think differently in a posthuman world and, above all, they do that through a change in their main channels of reproduction and collectors of mass and influence, namely the framing ley lines of infrastructure (Borch, 2014). They have to do much more *frame-work*. In these new urban ecologies or atmospheres, humans will have to stop seeing the world as an object exclusively laid out for their use. That is a refrain much heard but still rarely acted upon because the subject is still thought of as in opposition to the object rather than in symbiosis with it (or even parasitizing on it). But gradually we are coming to a new appreciation of objects which sees them as equal not opposite actors. In turn, such a view has consequences. Most particularly, it has an impact on how we think of politics. If the world speaks back not from out or over there but from in here, then we find ourselves in a different situation, one in which all manner of beings are or can be enfranchised even though that enfranchisement may not be equal. At the same time, fixed political positions are muddled up, since very little breathing space is given to a 'truth politics' of either left or right, one which is convinced that it knows what reality is and equally that all features of reality that do not fit this model are either needless and heedless or downright malicious ideological baggage (Harman, 2014). Everything is either known or potentially known in truth politics. There is nothing else to be heard that doesn't already fit. The standard kind of truth politics of both left and right fixes on moral absolutes declaratively displayed like a baboon's rump.[2] But the world isn't like that. Lots of things about it, including sometimes even the object of politics, cannot be known except in the practising of them. There are all kinds of objects not currently recognized by the collective that could become potent. But to know that, we don't so much have to wait and see as work it out, step by step. There is nothing necessarily wrong in acknowledging political ignorance. Indeed, it may be the foundation of 'true' political progress.

So what might our method be when we understand the city as more than human, as not just about 'subjective access', as Meillassoux (2008, p. 1) famously put it, and as therefore not just about a human-only politics but about a politics of decisions frozen in time and still reverberating through the serried ranks of infrastructure? As Graeber (2015, p. 36) puts it: 'the landscape surrounding major cities is peppered with the futuristic visions of past generations now lying smelly, dirty, or abandoned'. But how are political decisions calculated when vulnerability and decay are bywords and not just incidentals? What, in other words, would a *politics* of infrastructure look like? There are multiple possibilities, of course, of which we will offer up six.

First, there is a straightforward political task: to make the work of infrastructure repair and maintenance more visible, to make 'business as usual' unusual by moving to a new 'optical field' (Chattopadhyay, 2012) in which infrastructure not only has a politics but is a politics. That is the path already taken by many authors, especially in cities of the South where what infrastructure there is still often remains, if anything, all too visible, not least because repair and maintenance are often attenuated.[3] In turn, it is possible to consider all of the ways in which infrastructure can be undone 'so that we can make it possible to describe how modern infrastructures are appropriated and gnawed at to generate linkages and exchanges that were not intended, but also pry open a window to a different conception of infrastructure' (Chattopadhyay, 2012, p. 248). In turn, that makes it possible to think about different uses of extant infrastructure from those originally planned. However, care needs to be taken. Too often, such an approach falls back on a celebration of social and cultural practices to which infrastructure is only invited after the event. It is much more difficult to produce accounts in which that is not the case.

Second, and relatedly, humanity will have to redesign institutions like democracy which are no longer fit for purpose, not simply because they do not include nonhuman actors but also because it has become increasingly unclear what democracy is or what it might be as the history of democracy has unfolded and as new political causes have been added in. We are beginning to realize our own political ignorance. As a raft of recent books has pointed out, democracy has become a moveable feast. Democracy has always mutated and it has always been in crisis: as Runciman (2013) has pointed out, it is difficult to find a time when someone wasn't pronouncing democracy's imminent demise, but equally it cannot be assumed that democracies will automatically muddle through each and every crisis thrown at them, even though there is evidence that they tend to be more resourceful than other political forms. For example, apart from various existential crises like climate change, there are also general internal tendencies like the decline of political parties which, although they may have been representative, have often proved nonresponsive to voters' concerns (Mair, 2013) – with one effect being that other institutions, like the law or the media, have taken up the slack. Such changes as these are often diagnosed as a part of a new regime of 'post-democracy' (Crouch, 2004) or even a media-saturated 'audience democracy'. Then, there is the sheer variety of different kinds of democracy that do many kinds of different political things. Many countries lay claim to being democracies but there are widely differing views on which actually are such beasts. Last of all, these democratic systems exist in different ways in space. There are obvious electoral issues like gerrymandering. But, as importantly, democracies exist with many different spatial templates, which can have very different political consequences, and these have become particularly pressing in cities as they take on quite different political forms, even in the same country (Katz and Bradley, 2013).

Adding in other actors to this already unruly mix hardly clarifies issues. Latour has argued optimistically for a multistoreyed and spacious 'parliament of things', which would allow greater representation (and presumably greater responsiveness) for all kinds of nonhuman entities, a project achieved through a new school of political arts which can bring together different kinds of actor *and* different means of representing them through ceaseless experiment. It is about finding ways of speaking well about matters of concern that means designing new forms of agora (Schmidgen, 2014). But it is quite difficult to follow what this project might mean in practice, especially since Latour has made the whole proposition more complex through an emphasis on modes of existence, although the general impulse of greater richness of description leading to greater political fruitfulness remains the same. But this optimistic project that spots agency in numerous relational combinations of actors rather than the actors themselves may be too optimistic. Cities show the rub. They rely on organized forms of cruelty to nonhumans in order to maintain their human momentum: cities are hungry predators on other forms of life. Though they are often celebrated for their general creativity and life force, this liveliness can only exist because cities are also death machines. Thus, the search for food shapes cities: by one estimate (Steel, 2009), they rely on a global hinterland at least one hundred times larger than their inhabited extent, a hinterland in which servitude and death, because of agricultural monocultures, dietary change,[4] habitat extinction and the general machinery of industrial killing, is a fact of their lives: cities have nearly always been built on the cries and screams and howls of dying animals (Philo, 1995), but those cries and screams and howls have now become just another brick in a commodified wall, famously described by J. M. Coetzee as an animal Third Reich. It is worth dwelling for a moment on the facts of food because they show just how far we would have to move in order to produce a parliament of things. Take just the case of the humble chicken, the 'vast majority [of which] inhabits a shadowy archipelago of enormous poultry warehouses and slaughterhouses surrounded by fences and sealed off from the public' (Lawler, 2015, p. 5). Subject to centuries of genetic sorting, by one account the chicken is no longer an animal but a technology with model numbers to boot, each model carefully engineered to suit each consumer market. No wonder that twenty billion chickens are living on the planet at any instant, a ratio of three chickens to every human and far outnumbering the world's cats, dogs, pigs, cows and even rats (Lawler, 2015). But most of them will live for only six weeks, as opposed to the natural life span of ten or even twenty years, and will never be able to manifest the oft times impressive cognitive abilities that recent research suggests that they may well have. Only the most hardened cynic would never question such a state of affairs, especially as more and more evidence of animals' cognitive abilities crops up. Cities are built by optimizing the selfishness of one species at the expense in blood and pain of many others. Sharing is not on this urban agenda.

Third, it must be about learning to listen to the whirr of infrastructure by making things that intercede in it. After all, the Anthropocene produces different questions that need to be answered and their grammar is the sometimes mundane, sometimes weird contents of cities. So far, we have only partly listened to what the Anthropocene, in all of its 'thingness', has been telling us, and in large part that means we haven't been listening to the questions posed by cities. But, at their best at least, cities point us towards 'a way of being human that is not coextensive with the person or the thing, or with the perpetual transfer between one and the other that we have appeared to be fated to until now' (Esposito, 2012, pp. 150–1). Instead cities can offer ways of living which, in opposition to purity, can provide infrastructures, which are open to multiplicity, plurality and plurivocity, alteration and metamorphosis, propagation, contamination and finally contagion. Cities and their populations survive through infrastructures, but there is no reason why these infrastructures cannot be

made to sway and twitch in ways which are no longer
under the aged thumb of the conservatively inclined paci-
fier who mistakes subjection for order, or the adolescent
whip crack of the revolutionary who mistakes incitement
for agreement and irruption for transformation (Lordon,
2014), or the casual cruelties of the security-entertainment
complex, intent on maximizing attention for its own sake
and almost as a matter of routine willing to stoke affective
powers which are means of producing passions like anger
or fear or sexual anxiety.

Serres (2014) suggests that what we need to develop is
a new breed of philosopher kings and queens made up of
scientists who will speak in the name of the earth rather
than faction. That may be too ambitious! But what we
certainly need is a new cadre of engineers who are able to
make landscapes that can wake up and smell the coffee, so
to speak; engineers who understand that infrastructure is
both procedural and political. These engineers would not
be politicians but they would understand that infrastructure is a part of political deliberation. Engineers have been
trained to act as solvers of problems but their training is
too narrow, too constricted. They need to link modes of
existence that have drifted needlessly apart: listening to
needs, designing new solutions, disseminating and per-
suading. What we need is something akin to urban philosopher kings and queens able to turn their hand equally
to concept and execution, able to manufacture both new
and exciting means of growing cities and the kind of
consent that is not conditioned in advance. Engineers who
are responsible, in other words, for making and mending
in ways which will no longer be able to be reduced to
stock disciplines, whether these be architecture, or design,
or engineering, or planning, or data science, or what have
you, or to stock responses (for example, that cities must be
'resilient', able to take in endangerment as a key element
of city systems (see Evans and Reid, 2014)). Instead, this
new breed would act as urban impresarios but anchored
to the values of mutual need and sustainability rather than

to the nonvalues of simple profit and the accompanying repetition of ruin. They would be attuned not just to the immediate problems – pressing as those undoubtedly are – but also to the geologic understood as an early sighting as well as deep time (Ellsworth and Kruse, 2013). If, as Adorno claimed, modern normative senses are atrophied, then we need to *build* our way out of the impasse. And we can.

Fourth, and relatedly, we need to change our infra-structures so that they do not just act as tramlines but provide much greater senses of possibility. That means, above all, changing the way in which cities act as present to the world, which means being determinedly adventur-ous: 'dance, dance, otherwise we are lost', as Pina Bausch put it in the 2011 documentary *Pina* by Wim Wenders. It is no easy thing to magic up this spark, however. Too often, grand ambitions are accompanied by trivial or nonscalable examples that provide a sense of anticipation that is then far too easily overturned, with all of the usual disappoint-ments and attainders. But, equally, the last thing that we need is more grand model cities or buildings hylomorphi-cally declaring their superiority. We need, instead, an art of relaying change modestly, even when it is on a grand scale, so that we can 'maximize the transactive capacity of the urban fabric' (Greenfield, 2014, p. 1). That means recog-nizing that cities are *active forms* in at least three ways. To begin with, it means understanding that cities grow organi-cally for much of the time, through small additions that gradually add up to a larger change or through gradual absorption of one form or function by another. Though there is simple teardown and destruction, there is also a process of growth and obsolescence that can be measured in centuries as buildings come but only gradually go or are transformed piece by piece into something quite different. Then, and relatedly, it also means not assuming that all change requires continual addition. Much change in cities is about skilled *subtraction*, about what Easterling (2014a) calls the 'ecology of removal', about decay, deterioration and destruction. That is not just a restatement of such theses as Schumpeter's notion of creative destruction or more general notions of accelerated obsolescence for purposes of profit. Rather, it is an acknowledgement that the new can grow out of the old through not just demolition but also practices like salvage, reuse and recycling (Cairns and Jacobs, 2014). Durability is but one part of the play of urban form. Last of all, it requires an understanding that not all innovations have to be technical. Many of them are social and allow often quite simple and unglamorous technical means to be used in new ways. Cities of the South have led the way in thinking about such possibilities by wresting the last drop of value from the straitened circumstances to be found in, for example, squatter settlements. They allow for new shapes to action by providing new forms of sociotechnical intelligence that can result in alternative ways of building cities. Latin America provides some of the best examples of this tendency in the new architectural forms that are being derived there.

Fifth, we need a new vision of the world that gives all things a constituency. Often, that has been argued in Latourian fashion as constituting the aforementioned parliament of things. But without radical changes in how humans describe the world, that will be a difficult institution to achieve. Such a redescription must be about more than multispecies storytelling (Haraway, 2011), though that is undoubtedly an important element. But it is not necessarily impossible to achieve, either. The reason is straightforward. Humans *have* thought very differently about the world, as both the historical and anthropological records show. Take the case of certain kinds of animism or totemism. Or take the case of the ecology of selves found among certain South American forest-dwelling tribes that make real the possibility that the forest thinks. These tribes live in an animate ecology of selves in which all beings are volitional. That requires making provisional guesses about the motivations of others, dependent on where they are situated in that ecology, an ecology in which relations can change dependent upon context: predators can be prey but prey can also be predators; animals can be persons but they can also be once upon a time persons in the guise of meat; and so on. 'An ecology of selves is a relational pronominal system: who counts as an I or a you and who becomes an it is relative and can shift' (Kohn, 2013, p. 119). Thus it is that 'the human' is defamiliarized and the uglier aspects of human dominion can begin to be neutralized.

Sixth, we need a way of injecting these changes into the strips of interaction that make up everyday life. We cannot simply stay in the heady heights of 'why'. We need to get down to street level and to the many moments of 'how'. That is why interactionist studies remain so valuable: they reason from cases (Becker, 2014). But what would an interactionist study of a city thinking look like? What

Monster

happens when things are allowed their say in a circulating mass? What new elements can come into being? The kinds of exactitude that are required give the lie to the idea that so-called global urbanization, which is clearly premised on a surge of infrastructure, necessarily tells the whole story about the spatial logic of urbanization (Brenner, 2014). Other cardinals still exist, directions that give direction but challenge abstraction (see Becker, 2014, pp. 23–9; Walker, 2015).

Conclusion

As the lifeworld is increasingly engineered, becomes increasingly infrastructural in all its dimensions, from the economic through the cultural to the political, so the stakes are raised. For example, life increasingly mingles, having been actively designed to do so at the genetic-cum-computational level as developments like metagenomics and associated technologies like CRISPR-Cas9 take hold and allow large-scale engineering of life to become something less than a fantasy. All kinds of developments are on the horizon as a result. At the limit, what happens if the passenger pigeon is revived, as has been mooted in some quarters (Rich, 2014)? Or other recently extinct species? Or, more likely, active genetic and epigenetic interventions to improve the human body which go beyond the kinds of developments we have so far seen? Then, relatedly, there is the increasing presence of physical implants directly into the body. In other words symbiosis and parasitism become the norm and the very real possibility of the knowing production of human subspecies through new infrastructures hoves into view.

Against this fervid background, if we are to fend off the unfolding horror of a humanity which pulps the earth and itself and make something *personable*, that is neither overbearing nor thin and mindless, perhaps we need to move into the realms of fantasy where we can imagine being together with infrastructure – and being against – once more. That is one of the reasons why the fictive and fantastical has become a focus of so much urban writing of late. The stylistic production of gaps and tears and pivots can help us to imagine other worlds. We don't have to be reductionist, we could be productionist (Harman, 2012), allowing different fusions and fissions to haunt us that generate profusion and cannot exhaust what they describe. This is about more than simple novelty of content. As Harman argues, it is about undercutting, it is about changing the background, it is about testing the skills of the apparently maladroit, it is about urging on the process of debilitating content. It follows that it is not enough to use fantasy as a simple substitution of one situation for another. Rather, it is about conveying a different kind of intentionality, one which often scrapes at the door of what we can understand, one which withdraws from or polarizes our gaze, and one which in other ways challenges not so much our understanding as the basis of our perception of what can and can't exist in the shade we can both see and not see.

Increasingly, it looks as if the fictive and fantastical is something that does separate humans from most other animals (Suddendorf, 2014). Our capacity to bloom is based on a certain kind of ga(s)p between the standard ape mind and us. The gap is twofold. First, our ability to imagine and reflect on scenarios that have not happened, at least as yet. Second, our drive to link our minds together. We are intensely sociable creatures.

It is in this fantasy that we can see parallel cities opening up, cities which rely on infrastructures and resultant subject – objects we can only dream of but can give us pause and a means of changing the possibility that surrounds us. Consider the work of writers like Richard Jefferies, or H. P. Lovecraft and J. G. Ballard, or, latterly, China Mieville, or M. John Harrison, or Greg Bear, or Bruce Sterling, or Tony Ballantyne. They build and then devastate cities which are inhabited by things which have no regard for human welfare – indeed, sometimes they hardly register the human at all – and yet these cities are still inhabited by sentient beings, beings that are clearly intent on something – if only it were possible to divine what that something is. Their cities are involved in a constant metamorphic drizzle from one thing into others: suddenly changed forever, but we do not know how, fascinating to us, but we do not know why, wrapped up in becoming something else, but we do not know wherefore, weird, but we do not know to what end.

Understanding such cities might mean writing of the inner life of vast and monstrous agglomerations, frenzied and cosmopolitan or quiet and periurban. It might mean taking the measure of smaller cities that can be counted as 'provincial' or, just as easily, as bright and alert circles of friendship and common projects (Harman, 2012). Equally, it might mean writing of cities that have stepped out of the other side of the end of the world, blasted by war or environmental breakdown.

Whatever the case, in these writers' works cities *gain dimension*, and so does the human. They find a way of bringing life to Virginia Woolf's pronouncement that 'one cannot live outside the machine for more perhaps than half an hour'. That may be true, but in these works it is a fine half hour which marries speculation with anxiety and dread and an absolute love of storytelling through often allusive detail in order to produce something suffused with if not exactly hope at least a kind of longing or then again an extra load of entanglement or even a fascinated fear of what is around the corner, expressed in many different voices.

It is clear that what we find here is a reconfigured ecological impulse based on a degraded and continuous version of first contact. It is the urban version of Thoreau or Dillard, an ecology of fecundity and excess fit for places in which the naturalist tradition turns weird, based on a human transmutation and an ecocidal unravelling of infrastructure. Numerous modern works have tried to get at this transmutation. They all tend to be pessimistic, valedictorian in tone just as humanity seems to reach a pinnacle of success. There are the 'back to the land' moments of the Dark Mountain project; 'the machine is stuttering and the engineers are in panic. They are wondering if perhaps they do not understand it as well as they imagined. They are wondering whether they are controlling it at all or whether, perhaps, it is controlling them'. Better by far to look down to uncivilization than to look up to civilization. Better by far to look over the edge and cultivate an uncivilized writing.

> Uncivilized writing is not...environmental writing, for there is much of that about already, and most of it fails to jump the barrier which marks the limit of our collective human ego; much of it, indeed, ends up shoring-up that ego, and helping us to persist in our civilizational delusions. It is not nature writing, for there is no such thing as nature as distinct from people, and to suggest otherwise is to perpetuate the attitude which has brought us here. And it is not political writing, with which the world is already flooded, for politics is a human confection, complicit in ecocide and decaying from within.

Another way of considering what has been wrought can be found in VanderMeer's (2014a, b, c) Area X trilogy. Often understood as the depiction of a kind of natural extremity, a full speed ahead reversal of the Anthropocene, the opaque Area X might just as well be thought of as a reading of urbanity, of an 'unending wakefulness' (2014b, p. 155) in which everything turns into something else, a realm of pure infrastructure without beginning or end. Yes, Area X is a means of clearing the world of anthropogenic poisoning and then starting in on the human too (Tompkins, 2014). Yes, it is a biological machine. But, equally, it can be thought of as a reading of contemporary cities in which the human is in transition to something else.

> [The trilogy shows] us characters struggling to understand how their minds and identities might be changed from afar,

by systems of influence that they only vaguely understand. Ecology serves as a metaphor for the networked world – a world that's too big to comprehend, too pervasive to evade, and too hypnotic to resist.   (Rothman, 2015)

We can turn then to Watts' evocation of living fossils in an age when the human has shattered into many different subspecies as it is eaten up by infrastructure. Perhaps the biological-informational machines that it has brought into existence but which are now outpacing it are outdistancing the human. Pregnancy or cancer? Might or might not be living? Heaven or hell? There is no way to know, not least because awareness and self-awareness are separating out as informational infrastructure becomes everywhere, and wakefulness – what is live – becomes a question of yet and not yet. In certain ways, Watts is simply normalizing the actual diversity of life and especially its most extreme manifestations (Toomey, 2013). After all, so far as what counts as life is concerned, the anomalous is now regularly turning up as a norm. Science and fantasy have intersected. In certain other ways, Watts is simply asserting the importance of the continuing process of redefinition of redefinition.

As importantly, these attempts at fantasy all underline the importance of including what we have regarded as dead among the living – as living fossils, as practices whose original purpose has long been superseded, as memories which continue to cling on, as opportunities to turn the past into a different future. They bring us back, then, to the theme of infrastructure. Infrastructure provides the trails from the past into the future that, like the Australian dreaming, do not just locate us but tell us *what* we are.

Five Star Hotel

− 4 −
The Matter of Economy

As Bonneuil and Fressoz (2016) point out, when it comes to doling out blame, the Anthropocene is a differentiated phenomenon. Some parts of humanity bear a far greater responsibility than others for its advent. On one reading − theirs in large part − this can just be an excuse to get back to political economy as usual, devoid of all the actors who now have to be recognized as, well, actors. It's really the capitalocene (Bonneuil and Fressoz's blank incomprehension of what Chakrabarty (2009) is saying is illustrative). But on another reading, it is quite clear that the Anthropocene raises all kinds of issues of equity across not just human beings but all manner of other elements of the planetary combine.

Issues of equity are drawn in particularly stark relief in cities where human beings and others are most likely to be affected *en masse* (and where the more privileged are most able to take shelter from the coming storm (Stengers, 2015)). These issues don't just crowd together there, however, as if mass were just a matter of degree of emphasis. Because of the weight of urban infrastructure, cities have become a causative phenomenon in which the issues of economy and equity, infrastructure and species-being stand out like a sore thumb. More than that, even, they increasingly constitute an entirely original set of problems that require quite different kinds of solutions, solutions that challenge the hardened idealisms (of which – ironically – materialism is often one) that have become the contemporary equivalent of cynicism (Couture, 2016).

These issues are only underlined as the world becomes more and more urbanized, and the trails of infrastructure, defined broadly as modern machinic power, also tell what cities achieve and for whom. In this and the next chapter, we return to cities as composites to consider how the great matters of urban prosperity and poverty are settled. We say 'great' because world prosperity increasingly seems to depend on the capacity of cities to generate and circulate wealth, so the stakes are high, and also because cities are also the sites of concentrated world poverty, regardless of their character as growth engines. Here too the stakes are high, while the explanations of urban productivity and the recommendations to address urban poverty remain contested, and surprisingly negligent of infrastructure. First, we turn to urban prosperity.

Policy awareness of cities as engines of economic growth is fast rising. We see this in the reports of influential international policy and advisory organizations such as the OECD, World Bank, UN-Habitat, McKinsey and Company, and PricewaterhouseCoopers (PwC), among governments quickly realizing how much of the nation's economic fortunes and prospects are tied to urban developments, in the policy thinking of city leaders the world over, and in the locational practices of international corporations and institutions. Similarly, movements campaigning for social and environmental justice recognize that the fortunes of a world population concentrated in cities depends on their generative and distributive capacities. There is a growing sense among practitioners that the successes and failures of the economy may have something to do with the character of cities, offering more than the simple staging of otherwise independent economic processes.

This sense is confirmed by a body of scholarship on the economic benefits of spatial agglomeration (Scott and Storper, 2014; Storper and Scott, 2016). This writing identifies a host of benefits: the energy and entrepreneurship of the creative classes and pools of labour attracted to, or spawned by, cities (Florida, 2005; Glaeser, 2011); the specializations, savings and reciprocities enabled by industrial clustering (Porter, 2000); the market opportunities offered by urban scale and variety (Fujitsa, Krugman and Venables, 1999); the access firms have to public goods such as 'urban buzz', contact networks and public institutions (Storper, 2013); the gathered power of corporate headquarters, business and financial elites, intelligence vanguards and metropolitan leaders (Sassen, 2011; Taylor, 2013; Katz and Bradley, 2013). While opinions diverge on individual factors, the general consensus is that the competitive advantage of cities stems from the spatial concentration of people, firms and institutions constituting the supply and demand base for growth, efficiency and innovation.

This literature is not unqualified in its account of agglomeration. It also identifies a series of diseconomies, such as the costs of urban congestion, sprawl and overcrowding, and the negative consequences of infrastructural or institutional failure. Agglomeration is thus understood to require stewardship in order to reap economic dividends, through effective urban zoning and efficient circulation, sustained investment in skills, research and education, maintenance of the urban fabric, including its social and cultural facilities, provision for business clustering and collaboration, orientation of institutions and government towards collective urban goals, and generally effort to make sure that the urban territory, including its environmental quality, is properly managed. Increasingly, policy advice from influential organizations such as the World Bank, United Nations, OECD, and major consultancies such as PwC and McKinsey's is converging around these kinds of intervention to ensure that urban agglomeration can work for sustainable and equitable growth within and beyond the cities.

The literature on agglomeration chimes with our exhortation in this book to think of the urban as a force field, yet we do not believe that it is co-location that underwrites competitive advantage. One simple reason is that in the contemporary city characterized by urban sprawl, global flow and connectivity, networks of varying spatial reach, and colocation without contact, it is hard to know what agglomeration means, whether it yields the anticipated qualities, and if its returns are necessarily local. Cities are not clusters of linked markets, supply chains and business cultures, but assemblages of diverse economic logics and geographies with no necessary affinities at the point of intersection. The qualities of intersection – urbanicity – affect local possibility in each economic circuit in different ways depending on its overall spatial dynamic. The resonances of agglomeration are always mediated, folded into a wider force field. Thus it makes no sense to portray urban agglomeration as a set of spatial presences and absences that can be enlisted for growth, even if it were possible for policy makers to clear the knot of entangled spatialities that is the city to make way for better economies of proximity.

In this chapter we develop an alternative account of how cities influence economic performance. We focus on the additions and subtractions of the infrastructures that define settlement as urban and which mediate all economic transactions. We turn to the character, political economy and entanglement of road, rail and computer networks, water, electricity and waste disposal systems, calculating technologies and bureaucracies, buildings and habitats. Our argument is that this fabric influences urban economic performance – its quantities and qualities enabling, disrupting, amplifying, slowing down, and repeating urban economic potentiality. We see its power as directional, in the sense of a commons instantiating and sustaining the circulation of value. So, we turn to the qualities of this fabric in discussing urban economic policy, conceived less as the technical challenge of building efficient infrastructures than a political one of ensuring fair and sustained distribution in what is always the city of plural economic possibilities. Our focus falls on tackling infrastructural arrangements that only serve elite economic interests, on investing in maintenance and repair, since neglect disproportionately disables the smaller and weaker economic actors, on improving the distribution of public goods and services to socialize the costs of firms, institutions and employees, and on ensuring that service equity is designed into the ethos, technologies and logistics of delivery.

Water and electricity

Explaining Urban Prosperity

Cities are home to all kinds of economy. Work and value are generated in small- or large-scale manufacturing, in the utilities, services and bureaucracies, in markets, shops and warehouses, in the hospitality, leisure and tourism industry, in public administration and urban management, in urban maintenance and repair, in the provision of intelligence, education and training, in the money and credit industry, in housing and land management, in a host of business and commercial services. Each of these spheres includes diverse organizational forms, conditions of deployment and reward, qualities of distribution, opportunities for growth, capacities to survive, mixes of formality and informality, and modes of regulation. This variety increases as cities expand, become absorbed into transnational networks, scout for different markets and resources, and look for new means to gain competitive advantage in increasingly open and contested markets.

Because these ways of being increasingly involve flows of money, materials, information and knowledge from afar, along with transactional connections that stretch beyond a city, the performance of ventures located in a city can never be fully attributed to developments within the city. Even the value chains of small firms and artisan workshops now course beyond a city, as they become absorbed into longer retail, distribution and knowledge networks. So while the economic aggregates – the totals of output, employment, investment and profit – can be allocated to particular segments of a city's economy, a similar distillation of the drivers of economic performance is more problematic. This is because many factor inputs, business dynamics, and geographies of organization coalesce, and defy attribution to any growth formula applied to, or adapted for, the urban.

This is not to suggest that the sources of urban economic prosperity cannot be known. Instead, it is to be sceptical of essentialist distillations, either of all cities, or of individual ones: Bamako as all petty trade and rentier accumulation (ignoring the influence of national and international corporate power in Bamako); London as all high finance and hedonistic consumption (ignoring the usurious and informal); Bologna as all industrial clusters and craft knowledge (ignoring the growth of international finance and outsourcing). Such distillations have little bearing on real urban dynamics, yet they settle in quickly as givens of urban prosperity, guiding resource allocations and policy attention, privileging some cities over others. If it is true that 'accumulated wisdom of more than fifty years of research does allow us to state certain principles about the economies of cities' (Polese, 2013, p. 1), then principles such as the following five suggested by Polese bear a considerable burden of proof: a city's initial size and location, held to favour large, well-positioned conurbations; outside events or technological changes, held to alter a city's growth path and potential; the quality and reach of the transport and communications infrastructure; industrial structure and legacy, held to hamper adaptation and innovation if too specialized; and stable, transparent and efficient urban governance.

It seems intuitively correct that the large, diversified and well-managed city located in a gateway position stands a better chance of growth than the small, specialized city in a remote location plagued by foul air and foul play. But what is the basis of such deductive thinking, other than loose comparisons across time and space based on superficial observations and easy dismissal of the cases and conditions that don't fit? Are all five principles needed to secure lasting urban prosperity? Or is the corrupt and inefficiently governed city doomed to failure even if it complies with the remaining principles? Then, what about other conditions such as access to land and capital, the quality of human and social capital, the patterns of ownership and market behaviour, the economies of agglomeration and cooperation, the qualities and quantities of public goods and services, the rules of economic participation and regulation, the distributions of expertise, intelligence and social participation, and the legacies of urban design and planning? Beyond these questions concerning the grounds of distillation, the exercise itself sucks the life out of the urban economy by treating immanent conditions actualized in their doing in always situated and evolving ways as fixed determinants of urban economic performance, formulae for all cities.

City economies are far too variegated, interactive and immersed to be reduced to a standard set of drivers. This is not to deny the real differences in economic performance and potential between cities, nor to explain these differences as simply the product of local idiosyncrasies. London's economy is much larger and stronger than that of Bologna and Bamako, though its patterns of income inequality may be closer to Bamako's than Bologna's, whose micro-enterprises find themselves in a better business environment. Location, size, connectivity, variety and governance may well count in explaining the differences between the three cities, but so will other factors, and in the end it will be their combinations and actualizations in a transactional habitat unique to that city that count. This habitat includes the behavioural and cultural orientations of economic actors, institutional and infrastructural legacies, land, property and zoning practices, the amenities that attract and retain skills, businesses and professions, the facilitations of finance, credit and commerce, and the distributions of information and intelligence. The habitat defines the meaning and purchase of immanent economic conditions.

Key in this habitat is the infrastructural environment, for cities are, above all, constellations of entwined infrastructures, as we have been arguing. In addition to employing large numbers of people, generating value in their own right, and absorbing large capital investments,[1] these constellations map and visualize the economic field, enable and regulate transactions, shape preferences and expectations, maintain circulation and connect spaces, steer economic rewards and harms in specific directions, and provide the information and intelligence for economic decisions. They broker supply and demand, investment and profit, want and satisfaction, search and reward. The urban economy is both incomplete and impossible without the infrastructures that turn a settlement into a city. A conurbation *is* its overlay of infrastructures – the dense and interconnected systems incorporating buildings and spaces of transit and storage, technological and material networks, public utilities and services, transport and communications systems, and information and intelligence processing systems. These infrastructures hold a conurbation together and make it the machine that instantiates life in and beyond the city, including – it is our thesis – all matters economic. Markets are made, performed and sustained in the city through these infrastructures.

Awareness of cities as infrastructural machines is beginning to grow, aided by various visualizations becoming available of their sociotechnical systems. These include images of water, commodity and energy conduits, road, rail and flight paths, money, information and communication flows, disclosing the world as a web of cities connected to each other. Taken together they draw a world map showing the convening force of infrastructure, revealing the sizeable endowments of prosperous cities, often connected to each other, and the vulnerability of less prosperous cities and urban hinterlands dependent on securing access to these infrastructural webs (Brenner, 2014; Taylor, 2013). Infrastructural audits of individual cities are also emerging, along the lines of Kate Ascher's (2005) *The Works*, which reveals New York through the systems that move people and freight, provide energy, enable communications, and keep the city clean. Combining words, images and statistics, the book details the freight, anatomy and salience of the city's streets, subways and bridges, its rail, maritime and air networks, and its energy, communications and waste disposal systems (see also Robbins and

Neuwirth, 2009, for a historical mapping of the city's infrastructure). Such accounts make all too clear how much the fine balance between urban functionality and paralysis hovers around the amalgam of sociotechnical systems.

In technologically advanced cities, these systems are regulated by computational networks linking mathematical models, machines, experts and operatives continuously processing software-sourced information gathered from everywhere (Kitchin and Dodge, 2011; Shepard, 2011; Townsend, 2013). The smart infrastructures, as we discussed in the preceding chapter, allocate commodities, bodies, resources and information around and beyond the city, but also do much of the thinking and governing, arraigning human effort, rather than the other way round. From emerging visualizations of their spread into every nook and cranny of the city, it is becoming clear that these infrastructures are 'ontographs' of power – pushing, selecting, discriminating, bypassing, watching and engineering at a distance (Kurgan, 2013). The computer simulations, graphic representations, artworks and disclose the intelligence and agency of the meshwork hidden behind walls, under the ground, on the skin of the city, and in the air, as more than an adjunct, as more than facilitative (Thrift, 2014).

But more rudimentary and incomplete infrastructures are also ontographs, as is shown by a body of work that reads economy and society in cities of the South from their infrastructures. This scholarship reveals that basic supply infrastructures, such as those carrying water, electricity and sanitation, lie at the heart of a skewed urban political economy of urban prosperity and wellbeing – their incompleteness and terms of supply working for elites and middle classes at the expense of the urban poor (McFarlane, 2013; Ghertner, 2014). Equally, it shows that the patchwork improvisations of the poor, through technological piracy and cobbled-together materials, confirm the convening power of infrastructure, however rudimentary that power might be (Simone, 2014a; Sundaram, 2010; Larkin, 2013). The improvisations are held to mould social experience in quite profound ways, by dominating daily existence, shaping socioeconomic prospects, and making subjectivities and expectations long into the future (Graham and McFarlane, 2014). To think along these lines is to propose a different urban commons to that identified in the literature on urban competitiveness. It is to suggest that factors such as industrial clustering and collaboration, or abundance of institutions, intelligence and urban buzz are themselves instantiated by the urban infrastructure. Utopias of the city of the future have sensed this, with their often fantastical designs for transport and communication, housing and welfare, land use and settlement, the urban aesthetic (see Brook, 2013, for pivotal moments in the history of St Petersburg, Shanghai, Bombay and Dubai). They seem to have intuited that the qualities of the machinery of measurement, distribution, connection and amplification – let us call it urban automaticity – might be crucial for the urban economy. In the next section, we show how this might be the case, by exemplifying the strong and diverse dependencies that exist between infrastructure and economy.

The Substrates of Urban Productivity

To acknowledge the city as an infrastructural machine is to be open to its necessary presence in all sectors of the urban economy. If urban scholarship lags in recognizing this, that is not true of the international policy literature. For example, UN-Habitat, which has for a while campaigned for urban poverty reduction through social empowerment, income redistribution and trickle down of growth, has begun to think of streets (and other public spaces) as drivers of urban prosperity (UN-Habitat, 2013).

The organization claims that good transport mobility and connectivity in cities such as Paris, New York and London, which set aside a sizeable percentage of their land to streets and manage them well and for multiple uses, has secured higher economic returns for these cities by improving productivity, quality of life, social inclusiveness and environmental quality. Ease of movement and spatial connectivity in a large, dispersed and populated city are seen to yield considerable time, cost and welfare efficiencies for all economic actors and sectors – gains that are lost in cities with fewer, unconnected, and badly maintained or impassable streets. UN-Habitat concludes that although the streets of such cities may often host an array of informal economic activities, the suppression of general economic productivity and wellbeing is considerable (see also UN-Habitat, 2011).

Increasingly, the advice of the international organizations to governments and cities in the South is to bolster the economy through infrastructural renewal. Influential organizations such as the World Bank (2012) and McKinsey (McKinsey Global Institute, 2013a), recognizing the planetary significance of cities, are seeing stretched, failing or incomplete urban infrastructures as prime impediments to continued world economic growth and to the competitiveness of individual cities and countries. In the case of India, for example, the McKinsey Global Institute (2010) estimates that, amid their stark poverty and inequality, the country's rapidly expanding cities could by 2030 generate 70 per cent of net new jobs, 70 per cent of Indian GDP and 85 per cent of total tax revenue, along with quadrupling per capita incomes across the nation. To achieve this, the Institute recommends an eightfold increase in per capita infrastructural expenditure (an additional $1.2 trillion between 2010 and 2030) to bring the supply and quality of road and rail transport, affordable housing, and water, sewage and solid waste systems up to the required standard. India's future prosperity is unambiguously tied to the state of its urban infrastructure; a connection yet to be made in Indian policy thinking. McKinsey (2011) has made the same argument for Latin America. The state of the urban infrastructure is certainly central to the performance of global businesses. It is estimated that in 2010, some 8,000 companies were responsible for $57 trillion in revenue, the equivalent of 90 per cent of global GDP, with one-third of them headquartered in only twenty cities, where nearly 50 per cent of their global revenue is generated (McKinsey Global Institute, 2013b). By 2025, the number of companies with more than a $1 billion in annual revenue is expected to rise to 15,000, with much of the increase due to the rise of large companies from the emerging economies, run out of well-serviced 'home-base' cities. This set of cities hosting a small number of international companies will join a tighter inner ring of interlinked cities attracting many more corporate HQs and principal subsidiaries. This ring includes established world cities such as Tokyo, London, New York, Paris, Los Angeles, Singapore and Sydney, and new ones such as Beijing, Mumbai, São Paulo, Johannesburg, Kuala Lumpur, Shanghai, Buenos Aires and Moscow. Over and above company-specific city choices, such as loyalty to the 'home base', access to particular national or regional markets, and proximity to specialized inputs, these cities appear to be selected for their high-end infrastructures: fast transport and communication systems, collections of business, legal and media services, high-quality housing, social and welfare infrastructures, and the aesthetic of the urban landscape (Dicken, 2011; Beaverstock, Faulconbridge and Hall, 2014; Taylor, 2004).

Similar infrastructural offerings underpin high creativity urban ventures, be they the bohemian quarters of Berlin and Prague and the media and cultural industries of New York and Paris, or the high-tech clusters of Silicon Valley and Cambridge and the financial trading floors of Frankfurt, Hong Kong and London. The emerging economies have their equivalents in Cape Town, São Paulo, Buenos Aires, Rio de Janeiro, Mumbai, Bangalore and

Shanghai. These cities offer research laboratories and universities, entrepreneurial and creative individuals, cultural and media organizations, brokering intermediaries, and a variety of amenities and sites facilitating frontier explorations and risky collaborations (Florida, 2005; Storper and Venables, 2004; Scott, 2006). The social, cultural and institutional requirements of the creative economy are hard-wired into the urban fabric; for example, through the visibility of intermediaries that allow transactions to be made and closed, the intelligence coursing through smart buildings, technologies and communications networks, the infrastructures enabling search, mobility and connectivity, and a built aesthetic appealing to the creative classes. If the economy of Bangalore is held back in comparison to that of Silicon Valley or Cambridge, this may not be because the risk takers and creative people are missing or because the city's cultural milieu is somehow deficient, but because of infrastructural shortcomings, most obviously the city's ailing transport, communications, energy and water networks (Hollis, 2013).

But what about the 'ordinary' economy – the formal and informal activities servicing everyday living, maintenance and repair, the host of prosaic markets that sustain city life, soaking up far more enterprise and employment than the global businesses and creative industries? Largely ignored by the literature on urban competitiveness, this economy is the staple of the cities of the South and North. Any calculation of output and employment by activity and entity in a city will confirm this. The sheer presence in large numbers of humans, institutions, enterprises, buildings, infrastructures, technologies and real estate, explains the scale and significance of the 'ordinary' economy involved in urban provisioning, consumption and maintenance. While increasingly this economy draws on supply from around the world, its urban locations are no mere service or passage point, but instead a rich ecology of value creation and amplification with significant local returns. Many urban entities add to the supply chains, or operate independently to service the 'ordinary' economy. They often struggle to survive and face fierce local competition, but equally, they also draw on urban externalities and infrastructures to socialize their costs, facilitate transactions and enhance opportunity. In the circuits of the 'ordinary' economy, cities are spaces where supply chains are expanded in ways that contribute considerably to urban prosperity.

These amplifications are well illustrated by the urban dynamics of the off-the-books economy (informal, illegal, submerged, or nonmarket). The OECD (2009) expects the informal economy alone to employ two-thirds of the world's workforce by 2020. The off-the-books economy producing and selling every conceivable commodity is far from anachronistic or vestigial in contemporary capitalism. It is the fleet-footed link in the supply chains of the formal economy enabling profits to be concealed and costs to be reduced, it is the life-blood of the cities of the South (and the poorer parts of cities of the North), in equal measure meeting needs, generating value and perpetuating precarity, and it is the space of survival and experimentation in the social economy. This economy is a major source of global wealth creation, human resourcefulness and urban survival, ignored by economic theory. The urban ecology is an important stimulant and opportunity for it. For Ghani and Kanbur (2013), this comes in the form of agglomeration opportunities – spatial proximity, density and diversity, enabling small firms and enterprising individuals to find opportunity amid widespread want and poor economic regulation. For others, it comes in the form of skills learnt to negotiate habitat complexity, incompleteness and ambiguity. Robert Neuwirth (2011), for example, writes of the culture of 'stealth' in Lagos where services are sold in the gaps left by failed formal markets, infrastructures and bureaucracies, in San Francisco where internet intermediaries connect the needy to provisions in the social economy, in the majority of cities in which people jostle for a living where the poor learn to scour the landscape for opportunity.

Such accounts intimate a relationship between infrastructure and urban economic informality that is far from incidental. Think of the array of activities along functioning infrastructures, from the vigorous informal trading along busy roads, open spaces and transport hubs, to the maintenance and repair of utilities and public services. Think of the activities spawned by infrastructural failure providing pirated water and electricity to homes and businesses (Sundaram, 2010), building informal settlements (Holston, 2008), fixing motor vehicles and selling goods on congested and potholed roads (de Boeck, 2013), making good without mains sanitation (McFarlane, 2011; Thieme, 2013), sourcing food from informal markets, waste deposits, urban farms and disused green spaces (Tacoli, Bukhari and Fisher, 2013), selling counterfeit films, music and equipment (Larkin, 2004). In many cities, the do-it-yourself economy is the economy of incomplete infrastructures – its numbers immense though precarious, its habitat a space of improvised assembly (Simone, 2014b). So it is with the everyday formal economy of cities, where infrastructures provide the necessary public goods, accommodate businesses, institutions and workers, enable transactions, circulate factor inputs and commodities, join up markets, expand information and knowledge, and calculate possibilities.

Urban infrastructures instantiate and sustain the aggregates of the knowledge economy, specialist businesses and skills, and everyday formal and informal economy. Add to this their own contribution to urban output, employment and investment, and it becomes clear that they are key to urban economic performance. They are the automaticity that keeps things on the move, joins up the parts, lubricates the circuits, signals direction, provides collective intelligence, and shores up reserves in an otherwise open economy. They regulate far more than formal regulation, and they allocate and signal far more than the market. They are the summative force behind the dispersed and plural economic transactions of a city, the engine of innovation, prosperity and wellbeing – and their opposites, it has to be stressed. In cities, economy and infrastructure are closely intertwined. As sunk capital, infrastructure is just as lively as the most enterprising city actors.

A one-dollar ride

Meshwork Urbanism

In the urban age, the future of the world economy and the wellbeing of cities may well rest on the state of urban infrastructure. If development agencies are beginning to recognize this, national governments remain slow to do so, ensnared by market-led infrastructural allocations or the demands of the economically and politically powerful. They have yet to heed the concerns of the development agencies over the parlous and unequal state of infrastructure in the cities of the South, but also over the lag and mismatch between infrastructural demand and supply in the cities of the North. Perhaps they recoil at the recommendation that scores of trillions of dollars need to be invested over the next few years in urban and inter-urban road, rail, telecoms, energy, water, and waste disposal systems; investment considered essential to maintain world economic growth, for the reasons articulated above.

Infrastructure defined as the essential urban economic commons puts into question the necessity for urban competitiveness ria industrial clustering, knowledge concentration, collaboration between proximate firms, urban buzz and sociality, and other pets of the agglomeration literature. These projections of the dynamic of some world cities may prove to be far less important than generic infrastructural improvements such that cities can make the most of the plural vitalities, capabilities and markets within them. This is an economics of public goods built into the machinery of general urban supply, trusting in the potentiality of the enabled many, rather than in the engineering of economies of proximity. It attends to the basic substrates shared by a host of economic actors and entities, leaving different cities to build on their specific economic trajectories and spatial legacies. It deploys the language of infrastructural slack and redundancy, sunk capital and shared public goods, serving the urban economy by socializing costs, easing transactions and maintaining capacity (Ostrom, 2012).

If the economic logic of infrastructural urbanism is relatively clear, the practicalities and possibilities of intervention are not. The sums required by infrastructure-led growth seem staggeringly high, raising pointed questions about its likelihood. For example, according to the Africa Infrastructure Country Diagnostic (Foster and Briceno-Garmendia, 2010), approximately 15 per cent of annual African GDP needs to be invested on a sustained basis across the continent to bring about a step change in infrastructural quality and reach beyond the 7 per cent per annum currently spent, so as to mend broken and poorly maintained infrastructures, erratic and uneven water, sanitation and energy supply, and deficient transport, communications and logistic systems. This means an extra $100 billion a year – a figure close to or more than the GDP of many an African country – in a resourcing context in which the current two-thirds funded by national and local government is at the limit of toleration of further fiscal and tariff increases (Pieterse and Hyman, 2014). Such sums are beyond national reach, unless additional funding is made available by international investors and governments, who historically have exacted premiums and conditions frequently at odds with national economic and social interests. The infrastructural city finds itself trapped between hobbled or nobbled local institutions and self-serving or strutting international ones, none of them especially committed at a time of austerity to costly urban public goods without immediate profit returns.

Yet, this is exactly what is required, and could be made possible were an international policy consensus to emerge, brokering funds from various sources to underwrite an urban infrastructure-led Marshall Plan for global economic recovery; offering modest but stable long-term returns on investment that city and national governments and other public-interest organizations could access to implement properly audited public works programmes. Bolstered by other long-term funding schemes involving, for example, equity swaps, government bonds, philanthropy and public–private partnerships, the new Fund could nudge policy developments in quite decisive ways by underwriting a new model of urban economic preparedness. It would invest in decent and affordable provision of urban transport, communication, utilities, housing, learning and welfare, explicitly understood as the commons of economic productivity, and explicitly audited for its spatial and social reach. The attractiveness of potentially considerable sums of co-funding might encourage national and municipal authorities, along with private and international developers, to a model of economic growth based on the long-term urban infrastructure, in turn attracting further capital as its legitimacy grows.

This is the trace of only one possible funding model, but it shows that the financial challenge may not be insurmountable. Indeed, the greater obstacle could be the lack of interest in the model itself at a time of overwhelming policy commitment to short-term interventions with immediate market returns, and suspicion of the value of public goods – a situation that in many cities has meant planners siding with the vociferous, wealthy and powerful (Amin, 2013a). Our proposal may be judged as too generic, too indirect, too slow in picking winners in the hyper-competitive global economy, but only by ignoring the leverage provided in the city of many economic logics by the connective tissue: infrastructures operating as a meshwork through which things pass and connect, through which the city comes together as an entity, through which repetitions are secured and novelties channelled, and through which memories of the past and scripts of the future are stored (Weinstock, 2013; Amin, 2013b). The challenge for urban management lies in harnessing the collective agency of this meshwork and its arrayed objects, technologies, calculating devices, flows and intelligences.

This kind of re-provisioning would reinforce the intelligence base of the knowledge economy, the connections of the economy of cooperation, the sociality and serendipity required by the creative economy, the speed and reach required by the economy of the fast lane. It would also secure the services and utilities that an empowered and capable labour market requires, the savings and constancy of supply that allow small enterprises to survive, the basics that allow a social economy and other forms of economic experimentation to grow. Of course, each circuit will have its own specific infrastructural needs, but this does not negate the necessity of the provisioning baseline – set at an appropriate level for individual cities depending on need and available resource – because without that baseline the chances of each and every circuit are compromised. In short, meshwork urbanism invests in the infrastructure on a just-in-case basis, rather like the welfare state sought to do in the social arena of post-war Europe, investing in slack and redundancy to anticipate need and the unforeseen, and suspicious of just-in-time provisioning (Amin, 2014b). It does not look to place Darwin among the machines (Self, 2013) by trying to identify the adjustments that maximize fitness or adaptive efficiency (Weinstock, 2013, p. 23). There is too much variety, dissonance and emergence in the entanglements of the meshwork to allow this.

Olympics

Conclusion

Meshwork urbanism is more than a technical challenge, for urban infrastructures are far from neutral. They are political in every way: governed in favour of particular interests, biased in their affordances and allocations, shot through with calculative logics and mechanisms designed to distribute unevenly, and arenas of considerable power struggle. Most obviously, infrastructures are owned and run by monopolies that only too frequently make it their business to keep out new entrants, stifle competition, dissociate profits from service, and corrupt the rule of public accountability and interest. Investment and supply often follow the promise of money and influence, at the expense of people and places without means. The stories of infrastructural negligence, inequality and adventurism across the urban landscape are legion for these very reasons, as are those of pocketed profits, unmet needs and dangerous supply networks. If some cities and nations enjoyed a brief period of universal public service and capacious infrastructures, underwritten by high taxation, socialized costs and strict state regulation, this period has been seen off by a political economy of deregulation and privatization encouraging corporatist profiteering, while places that never courted universality continue to run systems that thrive on want and lack. Profit, power, ownership, regulation and infrastructural design are tightly interwoven – the meshwork made into a means of social and economic strangulation.

We can go further. Urban infrastructures are part of the biopolitical machinery – their material and routines settle and habituate distinctive regimes of social order and authority, and in ways that make the regimes seem natural, necessary, ordinary. They are the foreground and backfill of state historical projects and societal settlements, the key technologies of government incorporated into the everyday machinery of life. They are more than provisioning networks. Chandra Mukerji (2009) has shown this for the Canal du Midi, a pioneering seventeenth-century project that joined the Mediterranean to the Atlantic in Languedoc, France. The project, which the prevailing rituals of knowhow and patrimonial politics were unable to grasp, was brought to fruition with the help of new forms of collective intelligence, distributed reasoning and coalitional politics that eventually became emblematic of the emerging age of impersonal rule. In the transition to a new epistemic culture and a new politics, infrastructures such as the Canal du Midi displayed the 'uncanny power of things' (p. 203), the 'mute facticity' (p. 223) of locks, dams, barges and water flows habituating radically altered economic possibilities, social practices and governmental cultures.

In much the same way, Patrick Joyce (2013) and Chris Otter (2008) have shown how the infrastructural innovations of the Victorian period were central to the embedding of liberal rule in Britain. They consider developments such as the railways, the Post Office, the India Office, boarding schools, civic service, and new lighting technologies in the home, street and workplace, not only as facilitators of a mobile, communicating and visible society, but also as tools of the technostate, where government of the social order takes place at a distance, even at the farthest reaches, through the expertise, rationality, rules and rituals of these technologies. These developments are shown to have brought in a society of punctuality, luminosity, hygiene, connectivity, reach, orderly behaviour and a lot else; its material culture ordaining and making ordinary the powers, hierarchies and requirements of the liberal state. The service networks and their associated expertise, bureaucracy and artefacts, together with their provisions, became a habitus of organized freedom, as Joyce puts it. They legitimated the state as conduit and enforcer of the so-called free society, while scripting the principles of individual freedom, responsibility and self-management. The infrastructures of the Victorian age conjugated the liberal state as a cherished way of life, a mode of government that questioned the very idea of government while deepening its hold.

This kind of writing is careful to dispel any sense of infrastructures as the long arm of the state, unambiguously working for established centres of power and hierarchies of order. The networks of water, energy, transport, postage, lighting, training, education and civil service are shown to involve a host of repairs, innovations, breakdowns, improvisations and adjustments that deviate from the original intentions. They are shown to possess a life of their own and to sustain hybrid coalitions, evolving in their own right, often at odds with the centres of power. And they are shown to capture hearts and minds, domesticated by deliverers and users of services in ways that exceed, even subvert, the designs of the owners and regulators. This is particularly well illustrated by Stephen Collier's (2011) study of the infrastructures of the post-social state in Russia, showing how city officials committed to local populations facing severe adversity, but also old technologies built to serve large collectives (e.g. city-wide central heating systems), have defied the impositions of neoliberal urban management since the 1990s, finding a way around strict market principles of allocation to bring energy to houses unable to pay. Collier takes 'political reasoning as a situated practice through which existing governmental forms are reflected upon, reworked, and redeployed' (p. 19), to show that the governance of the post-Soviet social is anything but a mirror of planned intentions.

We can thus think of urban infrastructures as biopolitical machines in at least two senses: first, as the banal material of population management; and second, as life systems with their own motilities. Both can be seen as openings for an explicit and operative politics of government by infrastructure as a common-pool resource (Pennington, 2013). In the contemporary post-collectivist world, there is no momentum for making this shift. Its success, therefore, hinges on making public a common-pool infrastructural politics, exposing the biases and omissions of urban supply today, making visceral the benefits of universal access, spare capacity and social ownership and, more generally, agitating for the needs-based city and not only the profit-driven one. This is not a politics of technical fix, hoping that more and better infrastructure resolves the problem of skewed distribution and uneven economic service. Instead, it is a demand for a new kind of population management placing universal service at the centre of public under-standing of, and desire for, the good life, and pressing decision makers to organize the city as the public goods of the economy. It is a politics that requires active work to imbricate a felt sense of urban 'dead' matter as life-giving and economically empowering, and that nests protocols in the viscera of service systems to ensure fair and continuous supply, adequate maintenance and repair, and bias against profiteering from, and colonization of, the economy of public goods.

This politics looks to the subversive grain of existing infrastructures for added momentum, to the commitment of officials and operatives to principles of public service, to the many improvisations of the excluded to gain access to utilities, to the slack of just-in-case provisioning that troubles the precisions of just-in-time provisioning, and to reworking the hybrids that make up a supply network. The challenge is to find ways of proliferating these distur-bances, of making them count as valid and necessary. In the history of urban organization, there are some examples of economic positioning through infrastructural prepared-ness, for example London's history of infrastructure-led prosperity, starting with its mastery of shipping trade tech-nologies in the nineteenth century (Batchelor, 2014), and subsequently mixing a politics of zoning, planning, fron-tier technologies, and repair and maintenance to under-write the plural economy. It can be done.

Hunting

- 5 -

Frames of Poverty

If cities are growth machines whose intensities are regulated by their infrastructural conditions, they are also machines of marked socioeconomic disparity. In cities, wellbeing and want coexist, their interdependencies and separations maintained by the same meshwork of institutions and infrastructures. If this coexistence is widely recognized, the contributions of infrastructure, positive and negative, technical and biopolitical, are less well deciphered or agreed upon. This chapter focuses on the intensities and distributions of poverty, also traced to urban automaticity – the infrastructures of service delivery, welfare integration and urban access, but also on the framings and calculative logics of poverty. With the latter addition, we wish to show how infrastructure also operates as a system of inference regarding the measures and meanings of urban poverty and the methods of alleviation; its rituals and tools regulating perception of and response to the numbers and qualities of urban poverty in quite decisive ways. In the case of urban poverty, considering the frames of inference is especially important because they remain analytically plural and contested, as exemplified by the quotes below, yet normatively biased towards particular positions as we try to show in the chapter.

> Approximately 750 million people living in urban areas in developing countries were below the poverty line of $2/day, and 290 million using the $1/day line. This represents approximately one third of all urban residents ($2/day) or 13 per cent ($1/day), and one quarter of the total poor in developing countries. For the same time period, 2002, almost half of the world's urban poor were in South Asia (46 per cent) and another third in sub-Saharan Africa (SSA) (34 per cent) for $1/day line.   (Baker, 2008, p. 3)

> We find that the percentage of the population of the developing world living below $1.25 per day was halved over the 25 year period, falling from 52% to 25%...[by] slightly over 500 million, from 1.9 billion to 1.4 billion over 1981–2005' (Chen and Ravallion, 2010, p. 1598). [...] 'the developing world as a whole is on track to achieving the Millennium Development Goal (MDG) of halving the 1990 poverty rate by 2015. (p. 1600)

> The city is the home of prosperity. Cities are where human beings find satisfaction of basic needs and essential public goods. Where various products can be found in sufficiency and their utility enjoyed. Cities are also where ambitions, aspirations and other immaterial aspects of life are realized, providing contentment and happiness and increasing the prospects of individual collective well-being. (UN-Habitat, 2012, p. 10)

> Half the world's economic growth in the coming decade is projected to arise from cities in emerging economies. And most of that activity will transpire in the shantytowns and street markets of those cities. In this chaotic moment, the cities of the developing tier have an opportunity to define their own development paths. But only if the bottom billions have a voice. (Neuwirth, 2013, p. 4)

> Everyday lives in Africa's cities are to a large extent conceived around architectures that remain almost invisible

and are defined by lack and absence on a material level.
And many activities in the city become possible not because
there is a well-developed infrastructure available to sustain
them, but because that infrastructure is *not* there, or only
exists through its degradation and its 'absent presence'.
(De Boeck, 2013, p. 22)

We are witnessing the early stages of a shift from toilets as
fundamental citizen rights to gradually marketized commodities whose success depends on the entrepreneurial
capacities of civil society groups and small companies: even
bodily waste is not a limit-point to capital. (McFarlane,
2012, p. 2807)

There is not much consensus on whether world urban
poverty is increasing or decreasing, or whether cities exac-
erbate or better the chances of the poor. Organizations
such as the World Bank and UN-Habitat with the means
to measure world trends have been among the first to
reveal – and be concerned by – the concentration of large-
scale poverty in cities of the South (especially in South
Asia, sub-Saharan Africa and Latin America), yet they also
seem encouraged that numbers might be declining, as the
first two views of World Bank researchers suggest. This
optimism derives in part from the view exemplified by the
second two opinions that cities as engines of growth and
creativity offer opportunities to the poor to work, associ-
ate, consume, and make new lives in both the formal and
informal economy. In contrast, the final two observations,
respectively by ethnographers of the poor in Kinshasa and
Mumbai, suggest that life close up may be one of hardship
and struggle and systematic exclusion from the staples of
everyday life and the city's formal economic circuits. In
short, there is considerable ambiguity over the scale and
dynamic of world urban poverty.

Our aim in this chapter is not to resolve this ambiguity, precisely because the divergences of opinion are based
on clear differences of method and measure that end up
framing interventions and their evaluation. The canvas of

'truths' is part of the infrastructure – the machinery of knowledge production – reproducing and validating the truths, tying the proofs of achievement to the terms of assessment. All the more so because the canvas of truths is stacked towards particular policy stances. Accordingly, the chapter unfolds as an analysis of the discursive framing of urban poverty and the associated normative jostles and victories, all instrumental in making more or less of a methodology of numbers or qualities. We begin by looking at the effort since the 1980s to count the numbers – mappings of urban poverty at the world scale by international organizations such as the World Bank and United Nations, and at the local level by the poor and their advocates to make the case for recognition. We then contrast numerical accounting with in-depth research

Two dollars

on the lived experience of the poor in diverse urban settings in the developing world. We close by examining policy possibilities between the 'logics of calculation' and the 'logics of experience'. Aware of the limitations of standard policy solutions in addressing local specificities, yet conscious of the severity and obduracy of world urban poverty, we return to a politics of basic provisioning – the generalized supply of staples such as water, electricity, sanitation, primary health care and education, to underwrite the prospects and capabilities of the poor everywhere. We see no possibility of large-scale change without such a shift, one in which the principle and measure of the right to life and to the city returns to the discursive framing of poverty.

Logics of Calculation

International organizations measure extreme poverty by two lines: a lower line of $1 or $1.25 a day and an upper line of $2 a day. World Bank data (Chen and Ravallion, 2010) shows that in 1981, 1.9 bn people or 51.8 per cent of the population of the developing world lived below $1.25 a day, and 2.5 bn or 69.2 per cent lived below $2 a day. Estimates for 2005 stood at 1.4 bn or 25.1 per cent for the lower line and at 2.5 bn or 47.0 per cent for the upper line, suggesting a trend of declining absolute numbers and proportions of people suffering from extreme poverty. The trend, however, is skewed by developments in China, where the proportion of the population living under $1.25 a day has dropped from 84.0 to 15.9 per cent during the period, and that under $2 from 97.8 to 36.3 per cent. Elsewhere, both absolute numbers and proportions remain high, with half the population (391 million) in sub-Saharan Africa living under $1.25 a day in 2005 and eighty per cent (557 million) under $2 a day, and in India, 42 per cent (456 million) of the population living under

$1.25 a day and 73 per cent (828 million) under $2 a day. In Latin America and the Caribbean, and in the Middle East and North Africa, while the share of the population living on under $1.25 has dropped respectively to 8.2 and 3.6 per cent, about a quarter of the population still live under $2 a day (143 million).

These figures suggest that while extreme poverty may have dropped by a good margin in China and East Asia, and to a lesser degree also in Latin America and Arab countries, this is not the case in sub-Saharan Africa and South Asia, where hundreds of millions of people remain trapped in extreme poverty. The numbers, however, are far from undisputed. Reddy and Minou (2007), for example, cite alternative sources for Latin America, identify data inconsistencies between different parts of the world, and question the cost calculations of basic survival goods, to suggest that the scale of world extreme poverty actually increased during the 1990s, with World Bank figures overestimating the rate of decline in China and elsewhere. Sala-i-Martin and Pinkovskiy (2010), in contrast, confirm World Bank optimism, even for sub-Saharan Africa, drawing on PPP-adjusted GDP data from Penn World Tables to suggest that, although the $1 poverty rate for the region hovered at around 40 per cent between 1970 and 1995, by 2006 it had dropped by 10 per cent, coinciding with widespread GDP improvements, especially in the large economies of South Africa, Nigeria, Ethiopia and Congo-Zaire. Sala-i-Martin and Pinkovskiy's claim is that this largely unrecognized productivity growth has helped to bring down extreme poverty by improving participation rates and reducing welfare and income differentials.

The numerical ambiguity plays to, and performs, different positions on poverty reduction – celebrating or suspecting China's state-driven economic reforms, bemoaning or expressing surprise at African political economy, praising or condemning India's new-found liberalism. It reinforces pre-given positions on the relationship between economic growth and poverty and about the combinations of market, state and society required to reduce poverty. This is clearly evident in the recent history of mapping and interpreting world urban poverty. A decade ago, *Slums of the World*, UN-Habitat's (2003) first and influential attempt to calculate the world's slum population, portrayed a grim picture. The report forecast that by 2030, 50 per cent of the urban population – itself accounting for two-thirds of humankind – would exist on or under the $1 poverty line in slum-like conditions, largely in and around the cities of the developing world. The verdict of the report was unequivocal: slum life was, and would remain, a life of multiple deprivations, of few rights and even fewer reprieves, with inhabitants spending all their available resource and energy merely to survive.

Subsequently, the UN and other international agencies and consultancies, prompted in part by the severity of the forecast, have looked to improve data collection methods and more closely monitor developments. Recent UN-Habitat (2012) figures reveal, for example, that the developing world's slum population rose from a total of 650.4 million in 1990 to 862.6 million in 2012, which, taking into account higher rates of growth of the overall urban population, amounted to a decline in its relative weight from 46.2 per cent in 1990 to 32.7 per cent in 2012. This decline has been far from uniform, with the proportion of the slum population in sub-Saharan and many Asian and Latin American cities remaining persistently high, accounting for over 50 per cent of the urban population in Angola, Benin, Central African Republic, Chad, Congo, Cote d'Ivoire, Democratic Republic of the Congo, Ethiopia, Kenya, Liberia, Malawi, Mali, Mozambique, Niger, Nigeria, Rwanda, Somalia, Uganda, Tanzania, Zambia, Bangladesh, Nepal and Haiti (although down to 29.1 per cent in China, 29.4 per cent in India and 46.6 per cent in Pakistan, respectively affecting 181 m, 104 m and 30 m people). Taking the figures as a proxy of poverty (on the grounds that most slum dwellers live on under $2 a day and without adequate housing or services), the scale and extent of the problem of extreme urban poverty in the developing world remain considerable, regardless of the relative measures.

Interestingly, though, a decade on from its original publication, UN-Habitat has become more circumspect in its thinking. Its publications avoid long-term forecasts, note positive developments, and single out the countries of particular concern. While to some extent this shift reflects improvements in data and expertise, it also indicates a change in perspective on the city. The tone of *Slums of the World* was sober and urgent, presenting slums as badly-serviced and risky environments in need of sustained policy effort to improve access to land and housing, basic services, education, healthcare and connectivity. Five years later, in *State of the World's Cities 2010/2011*, UN-Habitat (2008) – still troubled by the scale of urban poverty and the exclusion of the poor in cities increasingly serving the haves – called on national and city leaders to commit to the poor on a human rights basis to ensure not only their access to the urban staples, but also their right to participate in a city's political and cultural life. However, the tone of *State of the World's Cities 2012/13*, published just four years later (UN-Habitat, 2012), is very different, and much closer to that of the World Bank (Baker, 2008), tying poverty reduction to urban economic growth and competitiveness. The language of rights has given way to a language of facilitation: to enabling the poor to participate in and derive benefit from the urban growth machine through reforms improving access to goods and services, jobs and opportunities, information and knowledge, and skills and capabilities. UN-Habitat too has adopted the prevailing policy approach to poverty (including elsewhere in the UN – see UNDP, 2010) influenced by the work of Amartya Sen (1989), privileging capability enhancement over rights and entitlements.

The logic of calculation is now full of interpretive ambiguity, raising important questions about the place of numbers in framing global urban poverty. With the numbers so uncertain, and filtered through distinctive normative frames, the truths of the calculative logic shift away from the facts. The facts seem unable to tell, for example, whether urbanization is exacerbating or ameliorating world poverty, whether China or sub-Saharan Africa is on the right tracks, or whether the urban experience – economic and infrastructural – helps or hinders the chances of the poor. Yet the uncertainties have not dented the calculative logic. Quite the contrary, for the data generated by the UN, World Bank and other international organizations, and the associated conceptual and policy inflections, have created a field of attention. Initially, it revealed that the dynamic of world economic and population expansion was associated with between half and three-quarters of the residents of most cities of the South living in slum conditions, on or below the breadline. The logic of calculation made visible the urban map of twenty-first-century mass poverty, and has subsequently informed proposals that interpret the numbers in their own way, to justify reforms of the kind outlined above as well as fuel warnings of dire consequences for survival, security and sustainability (Dorling, 2013).

The calculative logic has become pivotal in the field of urban poverty analysis and mitigation. From it arose the UN Millennium Development Goal to halve world extreme poverty (measured at $1.25 a day) between 1990 and 2015. The target, its monitoring, and the UN's claim that it was achieved by 2013, has allowed the rich sponsoring nations to define success by (blunt) numbers and uncontested indicators, to justify their approach focusing on debt relief and making aid contingent on market-oriented reforms, and to explain the inability of nations to meet targets as a failure to liberalize, democratize, rationalize governance. Calculation has become calculative, defining the actionable field and its measures of success, allowing gaps and anomalies to fall out of view, including serious underestimation of urban poverty resulting from ignoring the higher cost of living in cities, setting the income measures too low, disregarding living conditions and quality of life, and failing to recognize the specific challenges of being poor in the city (Mitlin and Satterthwaite, 2013). Similarly, the numbers have created a field of attention to which state and municipal authorities – increasingly under the gaze of international donors and regulators – cannot turn a blind eye. But once again, the numbers are selectively interpreted, aligned to governmental projects with 'intent' that frequently stray into the disciplinary when involving numbers-aided evictions, educational programmes, inclusion tests, conditional transfers, empowerment schemes, settlement decisions, and even sheer neglect.

The logic of calculation, as a viewing lens and stimulus for action, presses in on the poor themselves, posing a considerable challenge to their knowhow, resources and organization. But occasionally the poor mobilize it with good effect. Uncounted, the urban poor can only remain invisible, fragmented and ignored. The ability of communities to map undocumented slums and informal settlements is proving indispensable for the poor to be heard. These mappings are taking place, albeit slowly and under considerable pressure of failure, allowing slum dwellers to present their case and to be heard by the authorities, to contest official figures and the uses made of them (from evictions to service denial), to secure concessions from the authorities and gather resources for slum improvements, and to build links with other poor communities and their advocates (Appadurai, 2012a; Farouk and Owusu, 2012; Patel, Baptist and D'Cruz, 2012). The 'spirit of calculation', as Arjun Appadurai (2012b) describes it, has become an obligatory passage point in the politics and counter-politics of urban poverty. It serves divergent interests and agendas – this much is clear – but it is also the measure of their ability to make a significant dent on the reality of 1.2bn people living on under $1.25 a day and nearly 900 million people facing multiple deprivations in slum settlements.

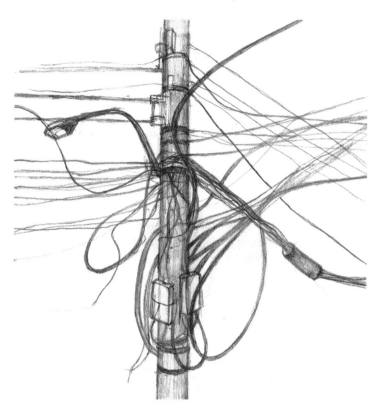

Ten thousand households

Logics of Experience

But in official hands the logic of calculation is also a blunt instrument, blind to lived conditions on the ground that intimate specific pathways out of poverty, inflected by local balances of social struggle, economic opportunity and political power. A growing body of qualitative research on slums and informal settlements shows that the logic of numbers soon dissolves into situated experiences – nuanced, place-specific and processual – that depart from the aggregated summaries. But in this literature too there are staples of reasoning about the experience of urban poverty around the world, with differential influence on policy practice. For example, UN-Habitat drew extensively on case evidence when it first summarized global urban poverty as a form of multiple deprivation: the exclusion of slum residents from adequate shelter, work, services, welfare, connectivity, safety and rights (echoing the tone set in Mike Davis's, 2006, pioneering book *Planet of Slums*). Now, the case evidence, selected in part to examine new thinking on cities as drivers of economic prosperity and creativity, is marshalled for a different framing of the urban poor, as subjects disconnected from the means of self-empowerment, a city's circuits of opportunity and growth, and urban participation in general.

Three narratives seem to be prevalent in case-based accounts of urban poverty. One, echoing the new UN-Habitat position, is a narrative of social endeavour and improvisation, acknowledging slum life as harsh and challenging, but also successfully negotiated by enterprising residents making home, neighbourhood and opportunity. This narrative avoids the hyperbole of blockbuster films such as *Slumdog Millionaire*, but it does not shy away from speaking of the resilience, inventiveness and achievements of slum dwellers. It discovers a vitality among residents, forever improvising, aspiring and persisting to tackle the difficulties posed by living in spaces of infrastructural absence (e.g. want, overcrowding, ill-health, insecurity, violence and harassment). The strength of this vitality, underpinned by entrepreneurial capability and honed resilience, is said to draw the line between destitution and wellbeing (Amin, 2013a). Two illustrative publications are Doug Saunders' (2010) *Arrival City* and Robert Neuwirth's (2005) *Shadow City*.

Arrival City is based on the journalist's experience of twenty of the countless number of settlements sprouting up every day on the outskirts of cities, which collect impoverished rural migrants driven into temporary shelters in search of work and opportunity. Saunders rejects the term 'slum' for its connotations of abjection and hopelessness, and finds in these grimy and ill-serviced clearances a populace teeming with rural craft skills and the drive to get on. The residents are seen as survivalists enduring adversity, mobilizing entrepreneurship, working with others to form businesses, finding work, making savings and building better homes, improving the fortunes of their children, and sending home remittances. Saunders sees these as 'transition spaces' from which the rural poor begin their journey towards becoming middle-class, drawing on their resourcefulness and social connections to get on, and, ultimately, move into better areas elsewhere in the city. He finds examples among Latin American favelas, Turkish gecekondu, Chinese 'urban villages', Dhaka's perimeter communities, all looser in their spatial and social morphology than 'blocked' settlements such as high-rise estates on the edge of Western cities, slums in the South in which the right to own or occupy is withheld, and settlements stifled by overbearing/corrupt authorities and populist organizations. Saunders proposes transition spaces as the self-help answer to mass poverty, supported by 'both a free market in widely held private property and a strong and assertive government willing to spend heavily on this transition' (Saunders, 2010, p. 288).

Neuwirth is another journalist also enthusiastic about the social power of 'squatter settlements', his term of preference. He criticizes slum clearance and re-settlement programmes for destroying the social ties and local familiarities he deems vital for surviving poverty. He argues instead for *in situ* upgrading led by coalitions of local residents and their representatives, and he singles out the right of occupancy as key to success (not the right of ownership, which is judged to be divisive and exclusionary). These findings are based on comparisons between four cities, allowing Neuwirth to claim that security of housing tenure – and recognition of this by the authorities – has encouraged residents in places such as Rocinha in Rio de Janeiro, Sanjay Gandhi Nagar in Mumbai, and the gecekondu of Istanbul, to invest in their properties, contribute to neighbourhood improvements, open businesses or find local work, campaign for municipal services, and participate in communal and associational life. For Neuwirth this is how over the years the settlements have become functioning neighbourhoods – spaces of residential improvement, communal maintenance, public participation, commercial development, and linkage with the rest of the city – providing residents with the means to lead fulfilling lives and to curate their neighbourhood. In the fourth city he studies, Nairobi, Neuwirth finds in contrast that settlements such as Kibera lack social enterprise and neighbourhood maintenance, because the absence of housing security (and collective organization) traps people in isolation, insecurity and hardship.

These are just two among a growing number of studies narrating slums as spaces of gutsy survival and social mobilization (with or without the right to land/housing). The turn in international policy on poverty reduction towards social capabilities thrives on such narratives, often playing down the persisting hardships and deprivations suffered by the poor because of policy neglect, the high price of essential goods and services bought from rudimentary and erratic incomes, the severe health and security hazards posed by overcrowding and poor living conditions, and the challenges of negotiating a sharply divided and unequal urban environment (Mitlin and Satterthwaite, 2013). It is oblivious to a second narrative that foregrounds the copious effort without guarantees made by the poor to stave off the miseries of poverty, lack and uncertainty. This narrative neither romanticizes the poor and their settlements, nor treats them as locked in abjection. Instead, it considers the poor as subjects with history and agency and the settlements as living ecologies, but in contrast to the first narrative, the stark imbalance between entrenched deprivation and fragile achievement is not ignored. It acknowledges the dynamism of life in slums but also the harshness and cruelty of daily existence.

A good example revealing the unpredictability and fragility of existence in slums is Katherine Boo's (2012) celebrated ethnography of Annawadi near Mumbai's international airport. *Behind the Beautiful Forevers* focuses on the precariously poised lives of determined individuals: a young breadwinner toiling against all the odds to corner a market in recycling household waste, eventually brought down by a harsh combination of happenstance and petty malice; an enterprising community leader who has risen through the ranks, shamed and exposed by the immoral demands of a vote-grabbing political boss; her daughter who manages to cling by the slimmest of threads to an education and teach the neighbourhood's children to read and write. Everyone is poised on the edge of, or mired in, extreme poverty and pervasive uncertainty. Boo shows that if Annawadi offers familiarities and favours that enable survival, it is also steeped in a culture of jealousy, animosity and patronage hampering social wellbeing and stability. A sameness of lack and frugality and an ambient uncertainty and insecurity press in on everybody, demanding skills of attentiveness and improvisation that work out for the most tenacious and enterprising, but never with any kind of assurance of consistency.

This dual nature of improvisation – its necessity but also its uncertain yield – is amply illustrated by other ethnographies. One is Ravi Sundaram's (2010) study of technological piracies in the poor neighbourhoods of Delhi in order to secure access to water, electricity, connectivity and entertainment. The inventive ways in which residents acquire basic services, search for opportunity, participate in the modern city, and enjoy the pleasures of music, television and radio are not exoticized, but treated as compulsions of infrastructural incompleteness – habits of improvisation learnt to secure basic services so that the harshness of their lack can be eased. Sundaram reveals the patched innovations as ordinary and everyday, simultaneously helping the residents to cope and presenting real risks in the shape of fast-moving vehicles in narrow streets, low-hanging live wires, dangers posed when the improvisations fail. Improvisation and inventiveness, in this case technological, emerge as necessities of negotiating infrastructural lack that are prosaic, facilitative and inadequate.

Philip de Boeck's (2013) writing on the improvisations of the poor on the streets of Kinshasa narrates much the same story. In the telling of survival in the interstices of this city of stretched and contested resources, de Boeck weaves in an old colonial office or radio station turned imaginatively by the poor into squats, marketplaces specializing in the sale of fried chicken skin to the hungry, vehicles adapted to carry dangerous loads, shades of trees on the highway occupied by a car-repair service and light from a private generator seized for a roadside café, and a cemetery claimed by street children left to live there as 'living spirits'. It is equally clear, however, that behind these improvisations and their remoulding of the city lies the reality of a state that does not provide, infrastructures that do not work, an exclusionary and intensely competitive informal economy, lack of housing for the city's predominantly poor population, and the merging of private and public space into a zone of indistinction. Inventiveness on the streets of Kinshasa is presented as a commonplace of survival, forced by radical uncertainty and constitutive lack, enabling the few who are lucky or wily enough to make a living and expand their orbit of security and influence, and the many without resources and support, to stave off hunger temporarily, illness and destitution. Like AbdouMaliq Simone's (2014a) imaginative account of neighbourhood making in Jakarta, there is no chosen tone of misery or romance in the telling, only the decision to encapsulate and locate social agency.

This narrative gets behind the 'capabilities' of the poor in under-served cities left to fend for themselves. Yes, it acknowledges the resilience of people shouldering burdens that elsewhere are absorbed by markets, states and infrastructures (de Boeck, 2012; Elyachar, 2010), as it does the ingenuity of people finding opportunity in petty consumption, recycling, and the many fleeting openings thrown up by pervasive informality (Thieme, 2010; Larkin, 2013; Neuwirth, 2011; Simone, 2014a). But it also shows how in conditions of instituted lack, uncertainty and hazard, these capabilities – and others painstakingly acquired through education, labour and experience – are constantly tested, are prey to misfortune, and fail to deliver lasting or general security. In settlements marked by infrastructural absence and intense competition over meagre pickings, the dissipations and disillusions of inventiveness are shown to be pervasive, and the thread spanning capability and achievement frayed. Little glory is found in the labour of the poor to survive, in the teeming life of the informal city.

If the above two narratives tend to focus on the lives and labours of the urban poor, a third one focuses on the mediations of politics: the rights of the poor, the actions of the authorities, middle classes and elites, the role of local and international aid organizations, the collective efforts of the poor and their advocates, and the structures of authority within settlements. These mediations, often underestimated in accounts focusing on social practice, are shown to be decisive in shaping individual and communal fortunes. The studies disclose differentials of state recognition that influence the poor's access to land, housing and public infrastructure (Chatterjee, 2011; Desai and Sanyal, 2012; Holston, 2008). They reveal the capture by middle classes and elites of the authorities and public opinion, leading to the resignification of the poor and their spaces as encumbrance (Ghertner, 2010; Aksoy, 2011). They show how the ability of the poor to stake a claim on the city rests on the quality of collective organization, leadership, and collaboration with officials and advocates (Patel, Baptise and D'Cruz, 2012; Roy, 2011; McFarlane, 2012; McQuarrie, Fernandes and Shepard, 2013). They reveal the damage done by well-intentioned international organizations misreading local needs or leaving implementation to usurious third parties (Satterthwaite and Mitlin, 2014). They uncover the hand of menacing and manipulating leaders, elected or self-appointed, working against the interests of the community as a whole (Boo, 2012; Truelove and Mawdsley, 2011; Ramakrishnan, 2015).

This third narrative traces the life chances of the urban poor to the contested politics of recognition and represen-tation: the play between international agencies, the author-ities and representatives of the poor and their opposites that determines the residential rights of the poor, their access to shelter, water, electricity and sanitation, and their chances of finding work, education, healthcare and safety. It looks at city and nation as a field of political struggle to explain, for example, why the end of dictatorship, together with sustained grass-roots mobilization in Latin America, has brought partial state recognition of the citizenship rights of the urban poor (as in post-Apartheid South Africa), why in India the citizenship rights of slum dwellers count far less than a politics of state concession, vote-catching, effective lobbying and self-organization, and why in the space of evacuated state and civic organization in many sub-Saharan countries, client, religious and kinship net-works – along with international aid interventions – turn out to be critical mediators of poverty.

Beyond these situated power plays, this narrative also tends to recognize a wider political trend worldwide of weakened commitment to the poor. It observes an aban-donment of past state promises to plan cities for general-ized access to housing, work and welfare, under pressure from population expansion, infrastructural and fiscal stress, and state capture by elites or market-led think-ing. Beyond the few countries still committed to central planning or welfare democracy, the politics of community is noted to have jettisoned the principle of universal wellbeing, or if not this, the assumption that the state should play a central role in securing the wellbeing of the poor. A political culture framing the poor as rights-bearing subjects with a legitimate claim on shared resources is thought to have given way to one treating the poor and their settlements as zones of exception: out of place, an encumbrance, a special case, a world apart. The upshot is a hit-and-miss politics of recognition that falls well short of providing for the poor, now contingent on the balance of force between competing urban claimants, generally stacked against the poor.

The logic of the argument is as follows. On the side of the powerful stand state and municipal authorities serving themselves or the middle classes and elites wanting the poor out of the way and the city organized to benefit their residential, business and lifestyle interests. The poor are heeded only when they organize, almost always on an ad-hoc and minimal basis, gaining a land or housing concession here, a public utility there (Amin, 2013a). There also stand the rich countries, international development agencies, and global consultancies interested in cities as business entities. The pro-poor interventions of this coalition are loaded with baggage: numerical targets such as the Millennium Development Goals failing to ask whether lives have been made better; aid projects ignoring the suggestions and innovations of the poor and tying support to changes in social or governance behaviour; parallel economic programmes worsening inequality, increasing prices and displacing the poor; the language of empowerment perpetuating an older legacy of 'rescuing' the South by saving it from itself, with all kinds of dependency in train. This is the political economy of good intentions in official international development aid (Mawdsley, 2012; Radcliffe, 2015).

Ultimately in this political economy, according to the narrative, the urban poor are left to defend themselves by bearing up, helping each other out, seeking out patrons and leaders, becoming organized. Some manage to pull through, and learn to fight for their rights, but many more remain down and out or are thrown back into poverty, exhausted by the effort required to organize in the harshest of circumstances, dragged down by the exacting conditions imposed by patrons and advocates. Organized self-help has become the means by which the urban poor can directly or indirectly access urban resources and the right to the city. This conditionality is not judged to be wholly problematic, especially in areas of Latin America and South and East Asia, where organization, advocacy and state receptivity have been strong, and where struggles have been backed by strong international slum alliances (Banerjee and Duflo, 2011; Satterthwaite and Mitlin, 2014; Appadurai, 2012b). Here, organized self-help is shown to have produced tangible benefits for the poor, along with building their capabilities. But it is also considered fragile, contingent on quickly exhausted communal energies, long periods of campaigning for small improvements that often fall into disrepair, sponsors distracted by other competing demands, and leaders struggling to maintain momentum. The successes are revealed to be hard-won, wearing and capricious, their extreme contingency no endorsement for poverty alleviation through self-help, marking the quiet passing of the right of the poor to wellbeing as an entitlement.

The narratives of experience stray in different degrees from an entitlements approach in recognizing the mediations of political economy and social power. They reveal the field of action and recognition to be plural and variegated – the right to the city contested in different measure between the poor, public authorities, private corporations, elites, client networks, political movements and pro-poor organizations. They restore history and agency to the poor and their settlements, seeing more than a jostle between rights recognized or removed, opening new options for a politics of provisioning for the poor.

Water supply

Frames of Action

The frames of action informed by the logics of calculation and experience, and their varied conceptual under-
pinnings, are encapsulated in David Satterthwaite and
Diana Mitlin's (2014) book *Reducing Urban Poverty in
the Global South*. The book identifies eight contemporary approaches to urban poverty reduction, some focusing on subsidies, infrastructural programmes and basic
rights, and others on markets, social mobilization and
patron networks (see Table 5.1). Satterthwaite and Mitlin
evaluate official initiatives such as national housing programmes and cash transfer schemes, municipal efforts to
upgrade slums, and international programmes focusing on
basic needs or empowerment. They also examine a host of
bottom-up initiatives and trans-local alliances such as the
National Slum Dwellers Federation in India, the Orangi
Pilot Project in Karachi, the Community Organizations
Development Institute in Thailand, the Asian Coalition
of Community Action focusing on East Asian cities, and
Shack/Slum Dwellers International.

Satterthwaite and Mitlin evaluate the eight approaches
by outcome, though their own preference – based on years
of research and advocacy in different parts of the world for
bottom-up initiatives and official programmes that engage
communities – is never far from the surface. Mindful of the
salience of the situated, they are careful to avoid blanket
policy proposals, such as local savings and microfinance
schemes or slum housing and infrastructure programmes.
However, equally mindful of the scale and intractabil-
ity of world urban poverty, they conclude in favour of
two general principles of intervention. One, deriving from
their criticism that the counting logic has underestimated
the scale and meaning of urban poverty in the South, is
to ensure that the poor are able to shape official policy
targets and initiatives. They argue that 'poverty can only
be reduced significantly when urban poor groups and their

Table 5.1 Summary of the eight approaches

Approach	Primary concern that approach addresses	Theory of change	Major concerns
Welfare	Assistance to those lacking the resources and access to services to meet their basic needs.	Establish the ability to provide cash or in-kind goods or services to alleviate immediate needs. Possibly make this conditional to change behaviour in favour of keeping children in school and attending healthcare. May be part-funded by compulsory individual and/or collective savings that helps to prepare for life-cycle needs and reduces the role of the state.	Achieving scale is critical but this is expensive and hence has to be a political priority. Programmes may tend to be top-down in management, dividing groups into deserving and nondeserving poor with discrimination against some groups. Some modes of delivery encourage the individualization of citizen-state relations, preventing the consolidation of social movements.
Urban management	Lack of planning basic infrastructure and services for urban wellbeing and prosperity.	Investment in infrastructure and services will increase income generation opportunities and support enterprise development. Those investments need to be located at the local government level to be effective. Evident need to manage land use and land-use changes guided by a city plan.	Emphasis on the management of urban centres for economic growth may lead to models of urban development that exclude low-income groups from the city centres and other prime locations. Modern urban management models may be expensive and unlikely to be an efficient use of scarce resources. Professional designs may be less effective for inclusive pro-poor cities than alternative approaches. The focus is the city, excluding consideration of the nesting of city economics within the macro-economy and social links at the household and other levels.
Participatory governance	Need for improved processes of democratic local government to ensure that it is more responsive to the needs and interests of its low-income and disadvantaged citizens.	Creating institutions of participatory governance to ensure that democracy becomes more pro-poor. This can be achieved through a diversity of strategies offering citizens and community organizations greater inclusion and influence in political decision making and state action. May extend to co-production.	Participatory forums can be limited in their decision-making role. They may also not be inclusive or pro-poor. Participatory opportunities may also be dominated by nonpoor groups, or include only some of those who were previously excluded. Government policies can be influenced by elites whatever the intentions of politicians. Clarity between models of representative and participatory democracy needs to be in place.

Continued

Table 5.1 Summary of the eight approaches (continued)

Approach	Primary concern that approach addresses	Theory of change	Major concerns
Rights-based	Failure of state to treat all nationals as citizens with equal rights. Failure of state to meet its duties and obligations.	Extending rights and entitlements will protect low-income and disadvantaged groups and individuals. The emphasis on rights rather than needs reinforces a broader understanding of social justice.	Rights can be difficult to achieve by groups that have little power. Legal processes to claim rights can be complex and formal, and hence exclude low-income households. Rights-based approaches strengthen the power and legitimacy of the state, which may be more concerned with property rights than the urban poor.
Market	Lack of access of low-income individuals and households to private services that have to be paid for, to market opportunities required to provide needed incomes over the life cycle and for enterprise development.	Improved access to financial markets will enable scarce cash to be used better to address needs and generate further income. The market encourages improved access to a range of goods and services. Often anticipated that an emphasis on markets will provide livelihoods opportunities.	Not all people are able to enter the market, and/or withstand the competition. Market approaches favour those who are already relatively better-off. Market approaches may increase vulnerabilities for households unable to manage debt. Does very little to address adversity in difficult macro-economic conditions.
Social and urban movements	Without strong mass organizations and associated processes to represent their political interests, the urban poor will be disadvantaged and will be excluded from political decisions and infrastructure and service provision.	Strong and capable urban poor organizations will be able to develop effective strategies and realize them. This includes making alliances with each other, building relations with a range of professional organizations, and negotiating with the state.	Movements respond to both immediate and long-term difficulties that the urban poor face. However, movement activities may be short-lived and with a focus on making demands on the state, and so may not sustain the pressure needed for substantive change. Movements may also be manipulated or co-opted by political interests. Movements may not represent the interests of the lowest-income members.

Continued

Table 5.1 Summary of the eight approaches (continued)

Approach	Primary concern that approach addresses	Theory of change	Major concerns
Aided self/help	The urban poor have to provide themselves with housing, basic services, infrastructure and land acquisition. They can do this better with the support of local government and access to financial services.	Individuals and groups make substantive investments in addressing their own needs for housing, infrastructure and basic services. With government provision of bulk supplies, trunk infrastructure, technical assistance, loans, and with appropriate regulatory regimes, much more can be achieved.	Without external resources and subsidies, the lowest-income households may not be included in the solutions promoted by aided self-help. Local solutions for improved basic infrastructure and services are unlikely to be fully effective without access to trunk infrastructure networks which require considerable state investment.
Clientelism plus	Lack of appreciation that clientelism provides an avenue for low-income disadvantaged citizens to access the state, albeit within vertical relationships that are often exploitative and which provide limited resources to some.	Clientelism does little for more of the urban poor than many more formal interventions. Recognizing the value of clientelist politics in assistance and access to land and basic services is important in developing pragmatic strategies for a more inclusive politics. Generally not an active intervention.	Glass half-full and glass half-empty debates may not recognize the insufficiency of the half-full glass. Hence, while clientelism does something to help some access essential infrastructure and services, it does not result in adequate services or adequate coverage. These practices reinforce vertical relations of authority and may be associated with violence and fear. The lowest-income groups may not benefit from the gains.

Source: Satterthwaite and Mitlin (2014, pp. 68–70). Reproduced by permission of Taylor & Francis Books UK.

organizations can influence what is done by the local and national government agencies that are tasked to support them, *and when* they have the space to design and implement their own initiatives and then scale up with government support' (op. cit., p. 239). Their recommendation is 'to build local organizations able to negotiate their way towards an alternative urban reality that works for the urban poor...from a position of strength whatever the nature and scale of the state' (p. 227). A sustained, worldwide, effort of community mapping, empowerment and federation is seen as the way forward, both in its own right and as a means of getting authorities to respond to the needs of the poor.

Secondly, Satterthwaite and Mitlin propose a reworking of the rights principle, arguing that 'for those whose realities are grounded in ongoing struggle against more powerful vested interests, legal rights are sterile, inflexible positions that are essentially inaccessible and which may never be attainable' (p. 226). Their focus falls on real rights protected through broader institutional guarantees that enable the poor to 'belong to groups and communities, to have a home that is safe and secure, and to have an identity that enables each individual to realize their potential...with safety, security and aspiration' (ibid.), thereby easing the labour 'realized in the lanes and alleys within informal settlements as people come together to work out how to improve their water, sanitation facilities, drainage, access to schools, health care, security' (ibid.). These safeguards are proposed as a right of 'universal access to *good-quality* basic services' (p. 248, original emphasis) – a right to be delivered by municipal rather than national authorities on grounds of jurisdiction and local knowledge. Satterthwaite and Mitlin recognize that municipal authorities are often hard pressed fiscally and operationally, but these constraints are seen as targets for reform, not reason to pass responsibility to national or international bodies.

In these two recommendations, the frames of calculation and experience are reconciled by proposing, on the one hand, generalized access to basic urban services, and on the other hand, the involvement of the poor in municipal decision making. We share this reasoning, though we are not convinced that municipalities can emerge as key players because of the very real financial and juridical constraints they face and because of their capture by elites. It allows for a critique of numerical logics, for example, of Millennium Development Goals and international aid conditions as hollow indicators of the real experience of urban poverty. It also allows for a general commitment to freeing the very large number of urban dwellers trapped in extreme poverty from the vicissitudes of happenstance and location. Like Mitlin and Satterthwaite, we vouchsafe this commitment including the right to basic urban services, but also formal entitlements such as income and welfare transfers. We have argued elsewhere (Amin, 2013a) that a binding global commitment to a portfolio of rights mixing different combinations of direct and indirect transfers, housing and land rights, and access to decent and affordable supplies of water, energy, sanitation and primary healthcare and education, is an essential step in securing the wellbeing of the urban poor on a lasting basis, without getting in the way of situated differences and granularities.

Contra Amartya Sen's (2010) claim that entitlements reinforce dependency and passivity among the poor, while empowerment measures encourage autonomy and self-help, we do not recognize the incompatibility, so long as a politics of rights proves to be enabling. State transfers in some developing countries to bolster the income or welfare of poor households by offering cash transfers or coupons for food, health or education, have been sufficiently parsimonious to encourage a dependency culture, yet the transfers have helped to keep destitution and disaster at bay (Sachs, 2005). Redistribution can be reformed to ensure access on a needs basis and without distortion, rather than rejected on dubious grounds of hindering market efficiency and social ingenuity (Easterly, 2006), encouraging wasteful and cumbersome bureaucracy (Collier, 2007), or even turning recipients into neoliberal subjects. The difference between the poor stuck in a precarious and abject existence and given the chance to improve their life chances may well have more to do with the terms of redistribution than with the principle itself.

The international consensus against entitlements between governments, development organizations and NGOs attracted by the capabilities perspective is premised on certain fictions of subjectivity – the freestanding individual or empowered community – and certain assumptions of organization – the provisioning market and functioning institutions – that are far removed from the contexts in which the poor find themselves. These presumptions play a cruel trick on a poor population yet to act in the expected ways and yet to witness the market as provisioning and institutions as enabling. They are a bad reason to cut out vital life supports. The scale of world urban poverty, exacerbated by appalling living conditions, incessant migration into cities, governmental neglect of the poor, elite colonization of resources and wealth, and multiple forms of violence including those caused by the unregulated markets, necessitates the return of a language of redistribution and entitlements that has been made unthinkable by a dogma of pared-back states, ubiquitous markets and entrepreneurial subjects. To think otherwise is to bask in the myth that the resilience and entrepreneurship of the extreme poor will suffice, and that it is possible to be better off without the support of institutions, public goods, redirected resources and asymmetric power within the city.

The right of access to urban infrastructure – the means of circulation, connectivity and provisioning in the city – is just as vital for the poor. Time and again, research on slums and informal settlements ends up revealing the crushing consequences of people lacking the bare essentials when there is no trunk supply, and the affordances created for work, wellbeing and security when a regular and affordable supply of basic services is available (Banerjee and Duflo, 2011). The sociotechnicalities and political economy affecting the quality and cost of access to housing, water, electricity, sanitation, and primary health care and education are shown to shape the life chances, identities and sense of belonging of the poor, to be the fault line of a future made or unmade (Amin, 2014a). They keep the poor from becoming substitutes for infrastructures by having to expend all their energy in meeting basic needs, and they stop providers and provisions of rudimentary available services from acquiring weight beyond the simple distribution of services. The character and quality of social life in the city, including the meaning of human potentiality, is formed in more than a coincidental way in the technical, political and cultural details of water and sewage, land and housing, schools and clinics.

Securing the infrastructures of basic need for some two billion people living on the breadline, mostly in the cities of the South, might seem like baying at the moon. These are cities with old and creaking public infrastructures that lack adequate repair and maintenance, bowing under the pressure of rapid population expansion and severe fiscal and financial stress on municipal authorities. In turn, their deficient infrastructures are organized by profiteering suppliers, cobbled together incrementally and informally, shot through with their own logics of operation, and claimed by powerful and influential interests. There is little incentive or margin to provide for the poor. The conditions of lack are ideal for providers and regulators to benefit from clientelist bungs and maintain the status quo, and to warn the poor to keep away from the city or make their own arrangements. Around lack and its infrastructures exists a hierarchy of interests and rewards, behaviours and expectations, averse to reforms designed to widen access to urban services.

This is not to give up on infrastructural reform in favour of the urban poor, made binding as a condition of

development aid. Funding and expertise made available
from a combination of governmental, private sector and
nongovernmental organizations – backed by an international infrastructure fund resourced from something like a
Tobin tax and stringently audited for service delivery to the
urban poor – could nudge municipal authorities towards
movements on the ground working with the poor to fashion
affordable housing, educational and health programmes,
and build decent transport, water, electricity and sanitation networks. If international consultancies working on
the infrastructural upgrading necessary for cities to drive
world futures anticipate the costs to be very high (Pieterse
and Hyman, 2014), their calculations take the legacy of
large, monumental and wasteful expenditure for granted,
including the absurdity of paying consultants and developers well over the odds to build fancy amenities and
infrastructures for elites and the well to do. Breaking with
this legacy would significantly lower the sums expended by
directing public money and international aid towards the
baselines of common wellbeing through incremental extensions of transport and communication, social housing and
slum upgrading, and public and welfare services.

   In any case, funding the infrastructural needs of the
poor need not be expensive, as shown by a raft of evidence from community initiatives around the world, especially those combining the expertise of experts drawing
on alternative or sustainable technologies and residents
crafting imaginative housing and service solutions from
limited resources (Aquilino, 2011; Parnell and Oldfield,
2014; Pieterse and Simone, 2014; Hernandez, Kellett and
Allen, 2010). The infrastructures produced – roads and
paths, meeting spaces, shared facilities, sanitation pits and
grey water ditches, water and electricity conduits, block
houses – cost a fraction of official expenditure elsewhere,
as does their maintenance and repair, relying on recycled
materials, pooled intelligence and communal labour. These
vernacular schemes could lie at the heart of urban infrastructure programmes, linked together by more expensive

integrative infrastructures to facilitate city-wide circulation and provisioning, in turn reducing the carbon footprint (Vince, 2014).

No pasarán

Conclusion

Critics will think it at the very least prosaic to end a discussion on urban poverty by focusing on infrastructural rights, or perhaps even severely mistaken in failing to tackle root causes such as inequality and asymmetric power. They might also think that the serviced city will simply attract more poor people into it and stretch resources, worsen congestion and pollution, and intensify competition. There is some truth in each of these criticisms, but we would also argue that in enabling the poor to build capability, and in endorsing the principle of urban public goods as a commons available to all, a politics of infrastructure prepares the ground for better opposition to the forces keeping the urban poor disempowered. Vested interests, embedded powers and exclusionary regimes will not give way unless forced to, and in an age when organized opposition to certain forms of market oppression is thin on the ground, the burden of change falls increasingly on the shoulders of the disenfranchised and their advocates. If, in the eye of this storm of political closure, infrastructural urbanism helps to build the voice, capability and coalitions of the poor as well as a city of more evenly distributed commons, its achievements will prove to be much more than prosaic.

At a minimum, a politics of infrastructural rights draws attention to the hidden, embedded, sites of power in the city organized as a sociotechnical machine, as we have tried to show in this book. Everyday infrastructures turn out to be crucial mediators and mediums of poverty and their innocuous actors, technologies, networks and conventions appear as anything but neutral in the distribution of urban opportunity and in the making of urban subjectivity. This actancy can be harnessed, though, for, as Keller Easterling (2014b) argues, 'infrastructure space tutors a shrewder, cagier counter to the lubricated agility of most global powers – an alternative extrastatecraft' (p. 23). If infrastructure space allows the 'real power players to maintain a currency in undeclared activities' (p. 22), working through the 'discrepant, fictional or sly' (p. 23), a counter-politics with more addressees and actors could begin to check these players out and hold them in check by mobilizing the same kind of sly powers. Such a politics adds a new frame to current thinking on urban poverty, currently split along lines of numerical or ethnographic reasoning and by preference for capabilities over entitlements. And in attending to the lively technologies that snake through the city with consequences for everything and everyone, it stands to deliver more than is normally assumed.

Systemic change

Epilogue

For this marvellous city, of which such legends are related, was after all only of brick, and when the ivy grew over and trees and shrubs sprang up, and, lastly, the waters underneath burst in, this huge metropolis was soon overthrown.

Jefferies, 1885, p. 38

Jefferies' apocalyptic vision of cities undone has figured large in many books and movies since. Now it is starting to look uncomfortably literal. This book has suggested that there may be ways, some already extant, others to be discovered, which might fend off this doom by thinking of cities as combinatorial machines, with their generative force derived in large measure from the character and composition of sociotechnical systems that provide supplies, information and intelligence, enable connectivity and circulation, bind together human and nonhuman, and amplify outcomes and resonances. We have argued that the 'extrastatecraft' (Easterling, 2014a) of such infrastructures, built environments, technologies and expertise plays more than an incidental role in shaping the dynamic of urban prosperity, poverty, sociality and environmental change. It follows that if we want cities to work for the common good, this machine will have to be governed in particular ways that skew infrastructure use in a project of general planetary reclamation

But this is no straightforward matter for at least four reasons. First, we have to understand that the machine is an assemblage of sociotechnical systems. Its agency is combinatorial and rhizomatic. It is not an art of precision engineering, as if such a thing were possible. It is not fully knowable or traceable, and its interactive character produces outcomes that are both recursive and emergent. Intervening in this environment requires finding switches and connectors that can amplify policy intentions and isolate damaging eventualities, but it also requires a premonitory intelligence and organizational flexibility that can keep up with the high degree of uncertainty to be found in such assemblages.

Secondly, we have to understand that the urban assemblage is itself a political machine – its infrastructures are 'de facto forms of polity faster than even quasi-official forms of governance' (Easterling, 2014b, p. 15). Sociotechnical systems have their own political economy, and that is precisely why the social and spatial distributions of public goods and services remain persistently uneven. Their upgrading is often a 'tool of governmentality that serves to sharpen and reinforce social inequalities' even in the name of renewal for the common good (Gandy, 2014, p. 222). But political economy is not a straightforward matter of ownership and control or the balance of redistribution and profit maximization, but one of prosaic compositional arrangements: the biases built into the algorithms, calculations, standards and technical configurations that drive the systems and their repair and maintenance (Amoore and Piotukh, 2015). The supposed technicalities of urban provisioning turn out to be an enormous political hinterland of access to resources, of proximity to and distance from contamination, of scripts of spatial and social selection written into objects which have broken out of the frames in which human thinking had formerly confined them. They call for the kind of over-reading and over-interpretation of automaticity that can make the urban machine work for the common good while understanding that the whole notion of the common requires radical reworking.

Thirdly, we have to understand that, at the same time, the urban machinery is not independent of more conventional forms of government. The definition and distribution of urban services – from utilities and communications to information and general infrastructural welfare – as public goods is influenced by how bureaucracies and decision or opinion makers frame the language and expectations of access and indigence, how governments and regulators expect suppliers to behave and systems to be maintained, how municipal authorities understand and deliver their own obligations and exercise their authority, how publics and communities understand the urban commons and their right of access, and how robust and effective the host of informal and improvised governance arrangements in the interstices of incomplete markets and bureaucracies prove to be. These sequences – and there will be others too – need to be managed in effective ways, raising difficult questions about who does the managing and how, in a regime of de facto distributed, differentiated and incomplete governance of the extensive city. If government is to remain, it has to be collaborative, strategic and inclusive, not panoptical. City leaders will have to learn to design the overall prospect with the help of many knowledge communities, to leave things to distributed vernaculars and capabilities but also to find a way of joining and amplifying them, to organize forums where diverse forms of expertise and intelligence can be mobilized to address common matters of concern but also to extract and sustain direction from the debates, and to manage the city's sociotechnical systems in ways that expand opportunity and benefit. In short, urban management has to become an art of conciliation and imagination, simultaneously directive and consultative, and always making adjustments, but without loss of traction. The management challenge is not slight.

Fourthly, we also have to understand that, at the same time, this combinatorial and polyphonic machine is taking on a 'life' of its own in the sense that it is beginning to go even farther beyond being a simple reflection of human cognition and is becoming something which continuously produces refractive potentials as part of a new settlement based on generating what Hansen (2015), following in the footsteps of Whitehead, calls a 'worldly sensibility'. We might say that cities 'think' in that through their changing form they produce various strains of efficacy that could not exist otherwise. But form remains an elusive quality. Because we exist inside it, 'form lacks the palpable otherness – the secondness – of a traditional ethnographic object because it is only manifest qua form in the propagation of its self-similarity' (Kohn, 2013, p. 185). Form is not about indexicality, the noticing and noting of difference, but about indistinction. Form is about day-to-day moments of interaction but it is also partially decoupled from them as pattern, recurrence, regularity. Form is fragile, but it achieves a partial order that is what we've got and what we work with. The politics of form will, we predict, become a major flashpoint, but because it is so difficult to find a language that encompasses it, it will also, because of this intangibility, remain opaque to any precise calculus of win or lose. It will never become 'a reformer's science or a Reason police' (Viveiros de Castro, 2015, p. 15). Rather, it will remain closer to an experimental art/science which is often unfettered from explicit intention but is able to 'think in men, unbeknownst to them' as part of a larger urban dreaming about what the future holds (Kohn, 2013). Sometimes, if we are lucky, we will be able to identify new and irreducible relational properties which can become new political holds, patterns of conjunction – and not just connection (Berardi, 2015) – which are something other than they were before.

The problem is that, in dealing with form,[1] we are dealing with terms – city, infrastructure – that are necessarily diffuse, dependent upon hierarchies of nested relations which both exceed and are continuous with their parts. That property makes tying down causality and agency a difficult challenge and can make etching out a politics an exercise in frustration. Cities are hybrids whose power comes from things brought together in more or less effective ways, partly through design and intent, and partly through the agency machined into the form of infrastructures themselves. Thus, there is bound to be a good deal of expertise put into articulating and aligning the different elements of cities, one still poorly grasped in the historical record, possibly because such a relational skill finds itself nested within other skills, which involve material intelligence, possibly because the only way to deal systematically with local complexity is to produce delocalized domains of expertise – batteries of skills – which can appear as modernist projects of transformation (Harvey and Knox, 2015). Yet in the historical record there are examples of cities that have produced a genuine municipal boost that benefits their populations by mobilizing infrastructure so that it is present in novel ways. They have spun new possibilities out of what looks like infertile tilth. We can think of new cities past and present that have planned for growth and contingency by designing capacious infrastructures and fairer systems of allocation. Constantinople, Delhi, St Petersburg and many new Chinese cities today come to mind, each with its own understanding of fairness. We can think of cities investing in future designs, intelligent systems, hardy maintenance and repair, appropriate mnemonics and powers of foresight to align infrastructures to changing needs and emerging stresses. In many senses, the history of utopian cities, and the contemporary interest in 'smart cities', are good examples. We can think of late nineteenth-century British cities mobilizing around the politics of water, lighting, sanitation and so on, to show that it is possible in improving mass wellbeing and what it is possible. We can think of contemporary cities with limited resources and technical or managerial capacity tying informal or vernacular infrastructural practices such as low-cost housing or communal sanitation into the wider urban grid in order to add to these practices. Brazilian urban integration measures focusing on public upgrading of informally constructed neighbourhoods are a case in point.

Of course, this is not a straightforward history of the common good pursued through a politics of mass provisioning. Sometimes top-down plans have turned out to be bland cul-de-sacs or rigid impositions, sometimes the curative effort and associated intelligences and resources have dried up, sometimes the turn to the informal and vernacular has become an excuse for doing only the minimum for the poor, and sometimes the expansions and renewals have been appropriated by the powerful and the vociferous to serve narrow ends. Above all, the infrastructural interventions have been political in their own right, with powerful coalitions of government, industry, regulators and investors often reaping huge dividends from engineering the city of mass provisioning, often at the expense of public service, especially towards poorer neighbourhoods and communities from whom only marginal returns are anticipated.

However, this is not a counsel of despair. What the examples also illustrate is the necessity of a series of combinatorial skills of construction, and their parsing into routines of maintenance, which, in today's city of hidden, multiple and distended infrastructural networks, will have to involve all manner of new forms of practical and symbolic diplomacy, expanded search capacities, creative compromises and coalition building ranging across a range of spaces. Inevitably, these skills bias towards qualities such as attentive and inclusive leadership, good project management, notions of good government, and so on – qualities that are often downplayed as minor political forces

(Harvey and Knox, 2015). To be clear, we see this skill set as less a matter of technical competence – though it is that – and more a matter of techniques of government which try to redefine what government might be. We are trying to point to a skill set that is able to align the numerous different and competing interests of city populations, through a judicious blend of bureaucratic and political skills able to produce unexpected alignments and cumulative effects through capabilities such as good timing, appropriate rhetoric, ability to leverage contact networks, and a realistic appreciation of the assets that any city has. City leaders – and that is a phrase that needs not so much redefinition as recasting as those who seek after interesting questions – need to know where the flow is, and to be able work in it and on it in productive ways.

Our central argument is that affairs of infrastructure need explicit government, capable leadership, and openness to a kind of multinaturalism, making room for a multiperspectival politics of existence in which infrastructural priorities become explicitly politicized, in which what are usually thought of as effects can become causes. In cities, given their rhizomatic ontology, this process requires connective capabilities, rather than those that flow from the arborescent logic typical of state power: skills of making the backyard into the front yard and then acting on it in effective ways, including with the most prosaic of interventions able to amplify or erode the powers that already exist. This is very different from the way in which classic governmental bureaucracies are supposed to work. For example, the ability to know what is required has to be bridged with the ability to listen, decentralize and be in touch. If city leaders once stumbled onto such techniques of urban government, today they need to work on them more explicitly if they are to direct the immense power and potentiality of urban infrastructures – towards the common good. The urban machinery can then become the ground of new bureaucratic procedures – a new 'utopia of rules' (Graeber, 2015) that attempts to stay light-footed.

These are also the necessary techniques of activism, for there is no intrinsic reason why city leaders should bend the urban machinery towards the common good. As Keller Easterling (2014b, p. 213) argues, redesigning disposition in infrastructure space requires the full range of 'sneaky' activist techniques such as 'gossip, rumour, gift-giving, compliance, mimicry, comedy, remote control, meaning-lessness, misdirection, hacking, or entrepreneurialism'. These stances mimic the power practices of infrastructures, produce a dialogue with the protagonists of 'infrapoli-tics' on their own terms, find effective ways of exposing narrow and divisive infrastructural arrangements, work on making alternative designs contagious and desirable and, above all, find ways of inserting new software and hard-ware into existing networks as multipliers of generalized wellbeing. These are the ways in which micro-experiments around the world for the urban common good – from mobile phone apps that facilitate money transfers in cities without banking, to low-cost public transport schemes and vernacular designs or co-ownership schemes for habitation – can begin to resonate. These are the ways in which the new is inserted into the old without turning everything upside down, and in which the vast networks of provision-ing can be nudged in new directions. These are the ways in which techniques of government can be scrutinized, challenged and eventually changed.

Such a politics of infrastructure is not incidental or reheated. If basic provision can be provided on a regular basis and to a certain standard, the many communities of a city come to possess the means to participate in city life in fuller ways. Such a politics is about preparing the ground for the more active participation of many communities – human and nonhuman, hybrid or multiple – in the life of a relationally verdant city full of provocation. It is about 'pre-truth' (Viveiros de Castro, 2015). This second order politics is of the first order when it comes to making imme-diate progress in the evolution of an existential pluralism that takes in the world and not just privileged elements of it and that considers understanding of the world as not just about multiple beliefs or perspectives but as about a transformation of, quite literally, the landscape of being and becoming. In this way, humanity is no longer positioned as the primary condition of life but rather as a half-being which must be blended with all kinds of other existences and their fields of sense (Gabriel, 2015) in order to be sustained – other animals, other materials, other senses, other symbolic properties. In other words, it is to acknowledge that this is a world populated by foundlings, a world in which everything is parented by others, a world in which relations become what counts as kith and kin but are continually cast asunder as they move into new formations. In a sense, all things start out broken and abandoned and have to be put together via uncertain processes of experiment and improvisation. This is an affirmation of an ontological incompleteness that allows for no sovereign force (Viveiros de Castro, 2011).

Recognizing the powers of infrastructure to not just contain but also provide possibility may only be the first step in this process of the creation of a humility which moves away from a humanist view of salvation and the politics that goes with it, but it is still a very important one (Stengers, 2015). It provides the stanchions – those sturdy but impermanent fixtures that provide the support needed to cordon off space in order to make it something more – that enable the possibility of a different existence to make its way into existence in the first place. Infrastructure is, if you like, the roots without which the tree cannot live. Its politics is therefore more than incidental. It cannot be – it must not be – sidelined. It is what, for better or worse, gives us the capabilities[2] to make transformations.

Notes

1 Looking through the City

1 One of the key problems is urban sprawl. Urban population expansion has involved suburbanization and the formation of megacities such as Tokyo, Lagos and Mumbai and mega-regions linking cities across vast distances (Ibadan-Lagos-Accra, Hong Kong-Shenzhen-Guangzhou, Mumbai-Delhi). Sprawl is a feature of urban expansion in the developing countries, where present high population densities (twice those in Europe and Japan and four times those in the USA, Canada and Australia) are expected to fall. One mapping exercise expects the doubling of the urban population of developing countries between 2000 and 2030 to be accompanied by a tripling of the built-up area of their cities (Angel, 2011). Thus, while the fashionable 'green' policy option of 'compact' cities, relying on infill, high-rise or multiple-use neighbourhoods to build the sustainable city of the future (World Bank, 2009), might be adopted by low-density cities in the developed world, it is likely to be resisted by rapidly growing, high-density cities in developing countries challenged by congestion, rising land values and irreversible sprawl.

2 These would include architectural or science fiction projections of the future city, ethnographies of the hidden or

vernacular urban, and films and novels that capture the mood of a city.

2 Shifting the Beginning: The Anthropocene

1 As Valverde (2012) points out, what counts as infrastructure is a variable quality. Thus roads have sidewalks and sidewalks nowadays often have trees, trees which can be highly regulated and may be seen as a hybrid of plant material and constraints on relative levels of mobility.

2 Although Smil (2013) argues that the global anthropomass – not the same thing, admittedly – now surpasses anything but bacteria in its presence by weight.

3 Bacteria can exist in almost any environmental conditions, including clouds: one cloud sample found 71 bacterial strains (Toomey, 2013).

4 But these stories of mass extinction need to be balanced out. New species also come into existence as mixing takes place. For example, ragwort has mutated as it has become a staple urban denizen (Pearce, 2015).

5 As an example, think only of the Pacific Northwest Cascadia earthquake, which is almost certainly gazetted to occur within a relatively short window of time along 700 miles of fault line. By one estimate, it will take between one and three months after the earthquake to restore electricity, a month to a year to restore drinking water and sewerage, six months to a year to reconstruct the major highways, and all of eighteen months to rebuild healthcare facilities (Schulz, 2015).

6 There is, of course, an alternative history to lifts. For example, the fire escape was introduced into New York in the mid-nineteenth century, becoming widespread in the early twentieth century. Since 1968 fire escapes have no longer been allowed in the city, but they have become such a fixture of its streetscape that they are now often the subject of landmark preservation disputes.

7 It is worth remembering that punctuation had to be invented. For example, the comma was invented in Venice circa 1500.

3 How Cities Think

1 Nowhere is this move better illustrated than in history, where climate change has become a serious explanans of historical change in stark contradiction to earlier accounts, which minimized its influence.

2 Equally, it is important not to opt for a politics of power in which the struggle is the only thing.

3 It is often remarked that the main problem in many cities of the South is not so much an ability to construct but an ability to provide systematic repair and maintenance.

4 And, in particular, the move to meat-eating in many parts of the world with its catastrophic environmental consequences (Steel, 2009).

4 The Matter of Economy

1 Vast sums of capital and debt, large numbers of people and bureaucracies, and long chains of supply and materials make up the world of urban servicing, circulation and settlement. The sums are not that much lower in cities with poorer infrastructures, since a raft of informal and improvised structures fills the gaps and failures of official and organized provisioning, however inadequately. It is the efficiency and quality of delivery of the infrastructures that will vary from city to city, rather than necessarily their relative weights in total urban economic output and employment.

Epilogue

1 Of course, the history of form is a long and complex one, wending all the way from Aristotle and Thompson to modern-day attempts to understand it as a vital property of worldly sensibility (Thrift, 2015).

2 The echo of Capability Brown's moulding of landscape is not entirely accidental. Brown declared that even the most barren landscape had 'capabilities'.

References

Ackerman, D. (2104) *The Human Age. The World Shaped By Us*. London: Headline.

Aksoy, A. (2011) 'The violence of change'. In Burdett, R. and D. Sudjic (eds.) (2011) *Living in the Endless City*. London: Phaidon.

Alexander, M. (2012) *The New Jim Crow*. New York: New Press.

Amin, A. (2007) 'Rethinking the urban social', *City*, 11, 1: 100–14.

—— (2012) *Land of Strangers*. Cambridge: Polity.

—— (2013a) 'Telescopic urbanism and the urban poor', *City*, 17, 4: 476–92.

—— (2013b) 'Surviving the future', *Environment and Planning D: Society and Space*, 31: 140–56.

—— (2014a) 'Lively infrastructure', *Theory, Culture and Society*, 31, 7/8: 137–61.

—— (2014b) 'Epilogue: the machinery of urban resilience', *Social Sciences*, 3, 3: 308–13.

Amin, A. and N. Thrift (2002) *Cities: Rethinking the Urban*. Cambridge: Polity.

Amoore, L. (2013) *The Politics of Possibility: Risk and Security Beyond Probability*. Durham: Duke University Press.

Amoore, L. and V. Piotukh (2015) 'Life beyond big data: governing with little analytics', *Economy and Society*, 44, 3: 341–66.

Anderson, E. (1999) *Code of the Street: Decency, Violence and the Moral Life of the Inner City*. New York: W. W. Norton and Co.

Angel, S. (2011) *Making Room for a Planet of Cities*. Cambridge: Lincoln Institute of Land Policy.

Appadurai, A. (2012a) 'Why enumeration counts', *Environment and Urbanization*, 24, 2: 639–41.

—— (2012b) 'The spirit of calculation', *Cambridge Anthropology*, 30, 1: 3–17.

Aquilino, M. J. (ed.) (2011) *Beyond Shelter: Architecture and Human Dignity*. New York: Metropolis Books.

Ascher, K. (2005) *The Works: Anatomy of a City*. New York: Penguin Books.

Ash, J. (2013) 'Rethinking affective atmospheres: technology, perturbation and space times of the non-human', *Geoforum*, 49: 20–8.

Augé, M. (2009) *Non-Places: Introduction to an Anthropology of Supermodernity*. London: Verso.

Baker, J. (2008) *Urban Poverty: A Global View*. World Bank, Urban Papers (5): Washington.

Ballantyne, T. (2013) *Dream London*. Oxford: Solaris.

Banerjee, A. and E. Duflo (2011) *Poor Economics*. New York: Public Affairs.

Basile, S. (2014) *Cool: How Air Conditioning Changed Everything*. New York: Fordham University Press.

Batchelor, R. (2014) *London: The Selden Map and the Making of a Global City, 1549–1689*. Chicago: Chicago University Press.

Batty, M. (2005) *Cities and Complexity*. Cambridge, MA: MIT Press.

—— (2013) *The New Science of Cities*. Cambridge, MA: MIT Press.

Bear, G. (2008) *City at the End of Time*. London: Gollancz.

Beaverstock, J., Faulconbridge, J. and S. Hall (2014) *The Globalization of Executive Search: Professional Services Strategy and Dynamics in the Contemporary World*. London: Routledge.

Becker, H. (2014) *What About Mozart? What About Murder? Reasoning From Cases*. Chicago: University of Chicago Press.

Berardi, F. (2015) *And: Phenomenology of the End*. New York: Semiotext(e).

Berlant, L. (2011) *Cruel Optimism*. Durham: Duke University Press.

Bernard, A. (2014) *Lifted: A Cultural History of the Elevator*. New York: New York University Press.

Berreby, D. (2006) *Us and Them: Understanding Your Tribal Mind*. London: Hutchinson.

Blokland, T. (2008) ' "You got to remember you live in public housing": place-making in an American housing project', *Housing, Theory and Society*, 25, 1: 31–46.

Bogost, I. (2012) *Alien Phenomenology or What It's Like to be a Thing*. Minneapolis: University of Minnesota Press.

Bonneuil, C. and J-B Fressoz (2016) *The Shock of the Anthropocene: The Earth, History and Us*. London: Verso.

Boo, K. (2012) *Behind the Beautiful Forevers*. London: Random House.

Borch, C. (2014) *Architectural Atmospheres: On the Experience and Politics of Architecture*. Basel: Birkhauser.

Born, G. (ed.) (2013) *Music, Sound and Space: Transformations of Public and Private Experience*. Cambridge: Cambridge University Press.

Brenner, N. (2014) *Implosions/Explosions: Towards a Study of Planetary Urbanization*. Berlin: Jovis.

Brenner, N. and C. Schmid (2015) 'Towards a new epistemology of the urban?', *City*, 2–3: 151–82.

Brook, D. (2013) *A History of Future Cities*. New York: Norton and Company.

Bryant, L. R. (2014) *Onto-Cartography: An Ontology of Machines and Media*. Edinburgh: Edinburgh University Press.

Bulliet, R. W. (2016) *The Wheel: Inventions and Reinventions*. New York: Columbia University Press.

Burdett, R. and P. Rode (2011) 'Living in the Urban Age'. In Burdett, R. and D. Sudjic (eds.) *Living in the Endless City*. London: Phaidon.

Cairns, S. and J. M. Jacobs (2014) *Buildings Must Die: A Perverse View of Architecture*. Cambridge, MA: MIT Press.

Callon, M., Lascoumes, P. and Y. Barthe (2009) *Acting in an Uncertain World: An Essay on Technical Democracy*. Cambridge, MA: MIT Press.

Castree, N. (2014). 'The Anthropocene and the environmental humanities: Extending the conversation', *Environmental Humanities*, 5: 233–60.

Chakrabarty. D. (2009) 'The climate of history: Four theses', *Critical Inquiry*, 35: 197–222.

Chamovitz, D. (2012) *What a Plant Knows. A Field Guide to the Senses of Your Garden – and Beyond*. London: Oneworld.

Chatterjee, P. (2011) *Lineages of Political Society*. New York: Columbia University Press.

Chattopadhyay, S. (2012) *Unlearning the City. Infrastructure in a New Optical Field*. Minneapolis: University of Minnesota Press.

Chen, S. and M. Ravallion (2010) 'The developing world is poorer than we thought, but no less successful in the fight against poverty', *The Quarterly Journal of Economics*, 125, 4: 1577–625.

Clark, T. (2015) *Ecocriticism on the Edge. The Anthropocene as a Threshold Concept*. London: Bloomsbury.

Cochran, G. and H. Harpending (2009) *The 10,000 Year Explosion. How Civilization Accelerated Human Evolution*. New York: Basic Books.

Collier, P. (2007) *The Bottom Billion: Why the Poor Countries are Failing and What Can Be Done About It*. Oxford: Oxford University Press.

Collier, S. (2011) *Post-Soviet Social*. Princeton: Princeton University Press.

Collier, S. and A. Lakoff (2015) 'Vital systems security: reflexive biopolitics and the government of emergency', *Theory, Culture and Society*, 32: 19–51.

Couture, J. P. (2016) *Sloterdijk*. Cambridge: Polity.

Crouch, C. (2004) *Post-Democracy*. Cambridge: Polity.

Cunliffe, B. (2011) *Europe Between the Oceans: 9000 BC–AD 1000*. New Haven: Yale University Press.

D'Efillipo, V. and J. Ball (2013) *The Infographic History of the World*. London: Collins.

Davis, M. (2006) *Planet of Slums*. London: Verso.

De Boeck, F. (2012) 'Infrastructure: commentary from Filip De Boeck.' Curated Collections, *Cultural Anthropology Online*, 26 November, http://production.culanth.org/curated_collections/11-infrastructure/discussions/7-infrastructure-commentary-from-filip-de-boeck

—— (2013) ' "Poverty" and the politics of syncopation: urban examples from Congo-Kinshasa', *mimeo*, Institute for Anthropological Research in Africa, Leuven: University of Leuven.

—— (2014) ' "Divining" the city: rhythm, amalgamation and knotting as forms of "urbanity" ', *mimeo*, Institute for Anthropological Research in Africa, Leuven: University of Leuven.

De Boeck, F. and M-F. Plissart (2004) *Kinshasa: Tales of the Invisible City*. Ghent: Ludion.

De Queiroz, A. (2014) *The Monkey's Voyage: How Improbable Journeys Shaped the History of Life*. New York: Basic Books.

Degen, M. and G. Rose (2012) 'The sensory experiencing of urban design: the role of walking and perceptual memory', *Urban Studies*, 49, 15: 3271–87.

Deleuze, G. and F. Guattari (1983) *Anti-Oedipus: Capitalism and Schizophrenia*. Minneapolis, MN: University of Minnesota Press.

Derrida, J. (2005) *On Touching – Jean-Luc Nancy*. Stanford: Stanford University Press.

Desai, R. and R. Sanyal (2012) 'Introduction'. In Desai, R. and R. Sanyal (eds.) *Urbanizing Citizenship: Contested Spaces in Indian Cities*. New Delhi: Sage.

Diamond, J. (2013) *The World Until Yesterday: What Can We Learn from Traditional Societies?* New York: Penguin.

Dicken, P. (2011) *Global Shift*. London: Sage, 6th edn.

Dobbs, R., Smit, S., Remes, J., Manyika, J., Roxburgh, C. and A. Restrepo (2011) *Urban World: Mapping the Economic Power of Cities*. Washington: McKinsey Global Institute.

Dorling, D. (2013) *Population 10 Billion*. London: Constable.

Douzinas, C. (2013) *Philosophy and Resistance in the Crisis: Greece and the Future of Europe*. Cambridge: Polity.

Dovey, K. (2010) *Becoming Places*. London: Routledge.

—— (2012) 'Informal urbanism and complex adaptive assemblage, *International Development Planning Review*, 34, 3: 371–89.

Drèze, J. and A. K. Sen (2013) *An Uncertain Glory: India and its Contradictions*. Princeton: Princeton University Press.

Easterling, K. (2014a) *Subtraction*. Berlin: Sternberg Press.

—— (2014b) *Extrastatecraft: The Power of Infrastructure Space*. London: Verso.

Easterly, W. (2006) *The White Man's Burden: Why the West's Efforts to Aid the Rest Have Done So Much Ill and So Little Good*. Oxford: Oxford University Press.

Ellsworth, E. and J. Kruse (eds.) (2013) *Making the Geologic Now. Approaches to Material Conditions of Contemporary Life*. New York: Punctum Books.

Elyachar, J. (2010) 'Phatic labour, infrastructure, and the question of empowerment in Cairo', *American Ethnologist*, 37, 3: 452–64.

Esposito, R. (2012) *Third Person. Politics of Life and the Philosophy of the Impersonal*. Cambridge: Polity.

Evans, B. and J. Reid (2014) *Resilient Life*. Cambridge: Polity.

Farías, I. (2011) 'The politics of urban assemblages', *City*, 15, 3–4: 365–74.

Farías, I. and T. Bender (eds.) (2011) *Urban Assemblages: How Actor-Network Theory Changes Urban Studies*. London: Routledge.

Farouk, B. and M. Owusu (2012) ' "If in doubt, count": the role of community-driven enumerations in blocking eviction in Old Fadama, Accra', *Environment and Urbanization*, 24, 1: 47–57.

Florida, R. (2005) *Cities and the Creative Class*. London: Routledge.

Foster, V. and C. Briceno-Garmendia (eds.) (2010) *Africa's Infrastructure: A Time for Transformation*. Washington: Agence Française de Developpement and World Bank.

Fregonese, S. (2012) 'Beyond the "weak state": hybrid sovereignties in Beirut', *Environment and Planning D: Society and Space*, 30, 4: 655–74.

Fujitsa, M., Krugman, P. and A. Venables (1999) *The Spatial Economy*. Cambridge, MA: MIT Press.

Fuller, E. (2014) *The Passenger Pigeon*. Princeton, Princeton University Press.

Fuller, M. (2011) 'Boxes towards bananas: dispersal, intelligence and animal structures'. In Shepard, M. (ed.) *Sentient City: Ubiquitous Computing, Architecture, and the Future of Urban Space*. Cambridge, MA: MIT Press, pp. 173–81.

Fuller, M. and A. Goffey (2012) *Evil Media*. Cambridge, MA: MIT Press.

Gabriel, M. (2015) *Fields of Sense*. Edinburgh: Edinburgh University Press.

Gandy, M. (2005) 'Cyborg urbanization: complexity and monstrosity in the contemporary city', *International Journal of Urban and Regional Research*, 29: 26–49.

—— (2012) 'Queer ecology: nature, sexuality, and heterotopic alliances', *Society and Space*, 30, 4: 727–47.

—— (2014) *The Fabric of Space. Water, Modernity, and the Urban Imagination*. Cambridge, MA: MIT Press.

Gandy, M. and B. Nilsen (eds.) (2014) *The Acoustic City*. Berlin: Jovis Verlag.

Gee, H. (2014) *The Accidental Species: Misunderstandings of Human Evolution*. Chicago: University of Chicago Press.

George, R. (2013) *Deep Sea and Foreign Going: Inside Shipping, the Invisible Industry That Brings You 90% of Everything*. London: Portobello Books.

Ghani, E. and R. Kanbur (2013) 'Urbanisation and (in)formalization', paper presented to World Bank's Sixth Urban Research and Knowledge Symposium, 8–10 October, 2012: Barcelona.

Ghertner, D. A. (2010) 'Calculating without numbers: aesthetic governmentality in Delhi's slums', *Economy and Society*, 39, 2: 185–217.

—— (2014) 'India's urban revolution: geographies of displacement beyond gentrification', *Environment and Planning A*, 46, 7: 1554–1571.

Glaeser, E. (2011) *Triumph of the City*. New York: Penguin Press.

Glennie, P. and Thrift, N. J. (2009) *Shaping the Day: A History of Timekeeping in England and Wales, 1300–1800*. Oxford: Oxford University Press.

Goffman, A. (2014) *On the Run: Fugitive Life in an American City*. Chicago: University of Chicago Press.

Graeber, D. (2015) *The Utopia of Rules. On Technology, Stupidity, and the Secret Joys of Bureaucracy*. Brooklyn: Melville House.

Graham, S. (2010) *Cities Under Siege: The New Military Urbanism*. London: Verso.

—— (2016) *Vertical: The City from Above and Below*. London: Verso.

Graham, S. and S. Marvin (2001) *Splintering Urbanism: Networked Infrastructures, Technological Mobilities and the Urban Condition*. London: Routledge.

Graham, S. and C. McFarlane (eds.) (2014) *Infrastructural Lives: Urban Infrastructure in Context*. London: Routledge.

Gratton, P. (2014) *Speculative Realism: Problems and Prospects*. London: Bloomsbury.

Gray, J. (2015) *The Soul of the Marionette. A Short Enquiry into Human Freedom*. London: Allen Lane.

Greenberg, J. (2014) *A Feathered River Across the Sky. The Passenger Pigeon's Flight to Extinction*. New York: Bloomsbury.

Greenfield, A. (2013) *Against the Smart City*. London: Do Projects.

—— (2014) 'The smartest cities rely on citizen cunning and unglamorous technology', *Guardian*, 22 December, pp. 1–7.

Guattari, F. (2014) *Lines of Flight*. London: Bloomsbury.

Hall, S. (2012) *City, Street and Citizen*. London: Routledge.

Hamilton, C., Bonneuil, C. and F. Gemenne (eds.) (2015) *The Anthropocene and the Global Environmental Crisis. Rethinking Modernity in a New Epoch*. Abingdon: Routledge.

Hansen, M. B. (2015) *Feed-Forward. On the Future of Twenty-First-Century Media*. Chicago: University of Chicago Press.

Haraway, D. (2011) 'SF: science fiction, speculative fabulation, string figures, so far' Acceptance comments, Pilgrim Award: Lublin, Poland.

Harman, G. (2012) *Weird Realism: Lovecraft and Philosophy*. Alresford: Zero Books.

—— (2014) *Bruno Latour. Reassembling the Political*. London, Pluto Press.

Harvey, D. (2012) *Rebel Cities: From the Right to the City to the Urban Revolution*. London: Verso.

Harvey, P. and P. Knox (2015) *Roads. An Anthropology of Infrastructure and Expertise*. Ithaca: Cornell University Press.

Hayes, B. (2005) *Infrastructure. A Field Guide to the Industrial Landscape*. New York: Norton.

Helbing, D. (2009) 'Managing complexity in socio-economic systems', *European Review*, 17, 2: 423–38.

Hernandez, F., Kellett, P. and L. K. Allen (eds.) (2010) *Rethinking the Informal City: Critical Perspectives from Latin America*. Oxford: Beghahn Books.

Heynen, N., Kaïka, M. and E. Swyngedouw (eds.) (2006) *The Nature of Cities: Urban Political Ecology and the Politics of Urban Metabolism*. London: Routledge.

Higgins, H. B. (2009) *The Grid Book*. Cambridge, MA: MIT Press.

Hillier, B. (1999) *Space is the Machine. A Configurational Theory of Architecture*. Cambridge: Cambridge University Press.

Hirschkind, C. (2006) *The Ethical Soundscape: Cassette Sermons and Islamic Counterpublics*. New York: Columbia University Press.

Hollis, L. (2013) *Cities Are Good for You: The Genius of the Metropolis*, London: Bloomsbury Publishing.

Holston, J. (2008) *Insurgent Citizenship: Disjunctions of Democracy and Modernity in Brazil*. Princeton, NJ: Princeton University Press.

Hommels, A. (2005) *Unbuilding Cities. Obduracy in Urban Sociotechnical Change*. Cambridge, MA: MIT Press.

Huang, Y. and E. Spelke (2014) 'Core knowledge and the emergence of symbols: the case of maps', *Journal of Cognition and Development*, 16, 1: 81–96.

Human Animal Research Network Editorial Collective (2015) *Animals in the Anthropocene. Critical Perspectives on Non-Human Futures*. Sydney: Sydney University Press.

Institute for the Future (2012) *2020 Forecast: The Future of Cities, Information, and Inclusion*. Palo Alto: Technology Horizons Programme.

IPCC (2012) *Managing the Risks of Extreme Events and Disasters to Advance Climate Change Adaptation*. New York: Cambridge University Press.

Jacobs, J. (2012) 'Urban geographies 1: still thinking relationally', *Progress in Human Geography*, 36, 3: 412–22.

James, W. (1977) *A Pluralistic Universe*. Cambridge, MA: Harvard University Press.

Jefferies, R. (1885) *After London, or Wild England*. London: Cassell.

Johnston, A. (2014) *Adventures in Transcendental Materialism. Dialogues with Contemporary Thinkers*. Edinburgh: Edinburgh University Press.

Joyce, P. (2013) *The State of Freedom*. Cambridge: Cambridge University Press.

Jütting, J. and J. de Laiglesia (eds.) (2009) *Is Informal Normal? Towards More and Better Jobs in Developing Countries*. Paris: OECD.

Katz, B. and J. Bradley (2013) *The Metropolitan Revolution. How Cities Are Fixing Our Broken Politics and Fragile Economy*. Washington: Brookings Institution.

Kearney, A. T. (2012) *2012 Global Cities Index and Emerging Cities Outlook*. Chicago: A. T. Kearney.

Kenny, N. (2014) *The Feel of the City. Experiences of Urban Transformation.* Toronto: University of Toronto Press.

Khan, O. (2011) 'Interaction anxieties'. In Shepard, M. (ed.) *Sentient City: Ubiquitous Computing, Architecture, and the Future of Urban Space.* Cambridge, MA: MIT Press, pp. 159–66.

Khanna, P. (2011) 'When cities rule the world'. McKinsey and Company, *What Matters*, 7 January (http://whatmatters .mckinseydigital.com/cities/when-cities-rule-the-world).

Khatchadourian, R. (2015) 'We know how you feel', *The New Yorker*, 19 January: 50–9.

Kitchin, R. and M. Dodge (2011) *Code/Space: Software and Everyday Life.* Cambridge, MA: MIT Press.

Kohn, E. (2013) *How Forests Think. Toward an Anthropology Beyond the Human.* Berkeley: University of California Press.

Kolbert, E. (2014) *The Sixth Extinction. An Unnatural History.* London: Bloomsbury.

—— (2015) *Field Notes From a Catastrophe. A Frontline Report on Climate Change.* London: Bloomsbury.

Kornberger, M. (2012) 'Governing the city: from planning to urban strategy', *Theory, Culture and Society*, 29, 2: 84–106.

Krebs, J. (2011) 'Risk, uncertainty and regulation', *Philosophical Transactions of the Royal Society A*, 369: 4842–52.

Kurgan, L. (2013) *Close up at a Distance.* New York: Zone Books.

Lancione, M. (2014), 'Assemblages of care and the analysis of public policies on homelessness in Turin, Italy', *City*, 18:1, 25–40.

Larkin, B. (2004) 'Degraded images, distorted sounds: Nigerian video and the infrastructure of piracy', *Public Culture*, 16, 2: 289–314.

—— (2013) 'The politics and poetics on infrastructure', *Annual Review of Anthropology*, 42: 327–43.

Latour, B. (2013) *An Inquiry into Modes of Existence.* Cambridge, MA: Harvard University Press.

Lawler, A. (2015) *Why Did the Chicken Cross the World? The Epic Saga of the Bird That Powers Civilization.* London: Duckworth Overlook.

Lazzarato, M. (2014) *Signs and Machines. Capitalism and the Production of Subjectivity.* New York: Semiotext(e).

Levinson, M. (2006) *The Box*. Princeton: Princeton University Press.

Levinson, S. C. (2003) *Space in Language and Cognition. Explorations in Cognitive Diversity*. Cambridge: Cambridge University Press.

Lieberman, D. E. (2013) *The Story of the Human Body. Evolution, Health, and Disease*. New York: Vintage.

Lindsay, G. (2010) 'The battle for control of cities', *Fast Company. com*, 16 December (http://www.fastcompany.com/1710342/the-battle-for-the-soul-of-the-smart-city).

Lordon, F. (2014) *Willing Slaves of Capital. Spinoza and Marx on Desire*. London: Verso.

Lorimer, J. (2015) *Wildlife in the Anthropocene. Conservation After Nature*. Minneapolis: Minnesota University Press.

McFarlane, C. (2011) *Learning the City: Knowledge and Translocal Assemblage*. Oxford: Wiley Blackwell.

—— (2011a) 'Assemblage and critical urbanism', *City*, 15, 2: 204–25.

—— (2011b) 'On context: assemblage, political economy and structure', *City*, 15, 3–4: 375–88.

—— (2012) 'The entrepreneurial slum: civil society, mobility and the co-production of urban development, *Urban Studies*: 49, 13: 2795–2816.

—— (2013) 'From sanitation inequality to malevolent urbanism: the normalisation of suffering in Mumbai', *Geoforum*, 43: 1287–1290.

Mackenzie, A. (2010) *Wirelessness: Radical Empiricism in Network Cultures*, Cambridge, MA: MIT Press.

McKinsey Global Institute (2010) *India's Urban Awakening: Building Inclusive Cities, Sustaining Economic Growth*. New York: McKinsey and Company.

—— (2011) *Building Globally Competitive Cities: The Key to Latin American Growth*. New York: McKinsey and Company.

—— (2012) *Urban World: Mapping the Economic Power of Cities*. Washington: McKinsey and Company.

—— (2013a) *Infrastructure Productivity: How to Save $1 Trillion a Year*. New York: McKinsey and Company.

—— (2013b) *Urban World: The Shifting Global Business Landscape*. New York: McKinsey and Company.

McQuarrie, M., Fernandes, N. and C. Shepard (2013) 'The field of struggle, the office and the flat: protest and aspiration in a Mumbai slum', *Public Culture*, 25, 2: 315–348.

Mair, P. (2013) *Ruling the Void. The Hollowing of Western Democracy*. London: Verso.

Malabou, C. (2008) *What Should We Do With Our Brain?* New York: Fordham University Press.

Manning, E. (2013) *Always More than One. Individuation's Dance*. Durham, NC: Duke University Press.

Marres, N. and J. Lezaun (2011) 'Materials and devices of the public: an introduction' *Economy and Society*, 40, 4: 489–509.

Massey, D. (2005) *For Space*. London: Sage.

Mawdsley, E. (2012) *From Recipients to Donors: Emerging Powers and the Changing Development Landscape*. London: Zed Books.

Meek, J. (2014) *Private Island. Why Britain Now Belongs to Someone Else*. London: Verso.

Meillassoux Q. (2008) *After Finitude: An Essay on the Necessity of Contingency*. London: Bloomsbury.

Merrifield, A. (2013) *The Politics of the Encounter: Urban Theory and Protest under Planetary Urbanization*. Athens: University of Georgia Press.

Metzinger, T. (2003) *Being No One. The Self-Model Theory of Subjectivity*. Cambridge, MA: MIT Press.

—— (2010) *The Ego Tunnel. The Science of Mind and the Myth of Self*. New York: Basic Books.

Mitlin, D. and D. Satterthwaite (2013) *Urban Poverty in the South: Scale and Nature*. London: Routledge.

Montagu, A. (1983) *Growing Young*. New York: McGraw-Hill.

Morton, O. (2009) *Eating the Sun. How Plants Power the Planet*. London: Fourth Estate.

Morton, T. (2013) *Hyperobjects. Philosophy and Ecology After the End of the World*. Minneapolis: University of Minnesota Press.

Mukerji, C. (2009) *Impossible Engineering*. Princeton: Princeton University Press.

Musser, G. (2015) *Spooky Action at a Distance*. New York: Scientific American/Farrar, Straus and Giroux.

Neuwirth, R. (2005) *Shadow Cities*. New York: Routledge.

—— (2011) *Stealth of Nations: The Global Rise of the Informal Economy*. New York: Anchor Books.

—— (2013) 'More telescopic urbanism, please', *City*, 17, 4: 510–16.

Nijhuis, M. (2015) 'What roads have wrought', *The New Yorker*, 20 March.

OECD (2009) *Is Informal Normal?*, March, Paris: Organization for Economic Cooperation and Development.

Ong, A. (2009) 'Intelligent city: from ethnic governmentality to ethnic evolutionism'. In Mayaram, S. (ed.) *The Other Global City*. New York: Routledge.

Osterhammel, J. (2014) *The Transformation of the World. A Global History of the Nineteenth Century*. Princeton: Princeton University Press.

Ostrom, E. (2012) *The Future of the Commons: Beyond Market Failure and Government Regulation*. London: Institute of Economic Affairs.

Otter, C. (2008) *The Victorian Eye*. Chicago: University of Chicago Press.

Parks, T. (2014) *Italian Ways. On and Off the Rails from Milan to Palermo*. London: Vintage.

Parnell, S. and S. Oldfield (eds.) (2014) *The Routledge Handbook of Cities in the Global South*. London: Routledge.

Patel, S., Baptist, C. and C. D'Cruz (2012) 'Knowledge is power – informal communities assert their right to the city through SDI and community-led enumerations. *Environment and Urbanization*, 24, 1: 13–26.

Pearce, F. (2015) *The New Wild. Why Invasive Species Will Be Nature's Salvation*. London: Icon Books.

Pennington, M. (2013) 'Elinor Ostrom and the robust political economy of common pool resources', *Journal of Political Economy*, 9, 4: 449–68.

Philo, C. (1995) 'Animals, geography and the city: notes on inclusions and exclusions'. *Environment and Planning D: Society and Space*. 13: 655–81.

Pieterse, E. (2013) 'Introducing rogue urbanisms'. In Pieterse, E. and A. Simone (eds.) *Rogue Urbanism: Emergent African Cities*. Auckland Park, SA: Jacana, pp. 12–35.

Pieterse, E. and K. Hyman (2014) 'Urban infrastructure, finance and affordability'. In Parnell, S. and S. Oldfield (eds.) *The*

Routledge Handbook of Cities in the Global South. London: Routledge, pp. 191–205.

Pieterse, E. and A. Simone (eds.) (2014) *Rogue Urbanism: Emergent African Cities.* Auckland Park, SA: Jacana.

Polese, M. (2013) 'Five principles of urban economics: things we know and things we don't', *City*, Winter, online version.

Porter, M. (2000) Location, competition, and economic development: local clusters in a global economy', *Economic Development Quarterly*, 14, 1: 15–35.

Radcliffe, S.A. (2015) *Dilemmas of Difference: Indigenous Women and the Limits of Postcolonial Development Policy.* Durham, NC: Duke University Press.

Ramakrishnan, K. (2015) 'Stalled Futures: Aspirations and Belonging in a Delhi Resettlement Colony', *Unpublished PhD Thesis*, Department of Geography, University of Cambridge.

Reddy, S. and C. Minou (2007) 'Has World Poverty Really Fallen?,' *Review of Income and Wealth*, 53, 3: 484–502.

Rich, N. (2014) 'The mammoth cometh', *New York Times Magazine*, 27 February.

Robbins, S. and R. Neuwirth (eds.) (2009) *Mapping New York.* London: Black Dog Publishing.

Rodowick, D. N. (1997) *Gilles Deleuze's Time Machine.* Durham: Duke University Press.

Rothman, J. (2015) The weird Thoreau', *The New Yorker*, 14 January.

Roy, A. (2011) 'Slumdog cities', *International Journal of Urban and Regional Research*, 35, 2: 223–38.

—— (2014) 'Worlding the city: toward a post-colonial urban theory'. In Parnell, S. and S. Oldfield (eds.) *The Routledge Handbook on Cities of the Global South.* London: Routledge, pp. 9–120.

Rubenstein, M. (2014) *Worlds Without End. The Many Lives of the Multiverse.* New York: Columbia University Press.

Runciman, D. (2013) *The Confidence Trap.* Princeton: Princeton University Press.

Sachs, J. (2005) *The End of Poverty: Economic Possibility for our Time.* New York: Penguin.

Sala-i-Martin, X. and M. Pinkovskiy (2010) 'African poverty is falling ... much faster than you think!', *Working Paper 15775*, National Bureau of Economic Research: Cambridge.

Sanders, T. I. (2008) 'Complex systems thinking and new urbanism'. In Haas, T. (ed.) *New Urbanism and Beyond: Designing Cities for the Future*. New York: Rizzoli.

Sassen, S. (2006) *Territory, Authority, Rights*. Princeton: Princeton University Press.

—— (2011) *Cities in a World Economy*. London: Sage, 4th edn.

—— (2012a) 'Beyond state-to-state geopolitics: urban vectors dominate'. In A. T. Kearney, *2012 Global Cities Index and Emerging Cities Outlook*. Chicago: A. T. Kearney.

—— (2012b) 'Urbanising technologies'. In Burdett, R. and P. Rode (eds.) *Urban Age Electric City Conference*. London: London School of Economics, pp. 12–14.

—— (2014) *Expulsions, Complexity and Brutality*. Cambridge, MA: Harvard University Press.

Satterthwaite, D. and D. Mitlin (2014) *Reducing Urban Poverty in the Global South*. London: Routledge.

Saunders, D. (2010) *Arrival City*. New York: Pantheon Books.

Sawhney, H. (ed.) (2009) *Delhi Noir*. India: Noida, University Press, Harper Collins.

Schmidgen, H. (2014) *Bruno Latour in Pieces. An Intellectual Biography*. New York: Fordham University Press.

Schulz, K. (2015) 'The really big one', *The New Yorker*, 20 July, 52–9.

Scott, A. J. (2006) 'Creative cities: conceptual issues and policy questions', *Journal of Urban Affairs*, 28, 1: 1–17.

Scott, A. J. and M. Storper (2014) 'The nature of cities', *International Journal of Urban and Regional Research*, 39: 1–15.

Self, J. (2013) 'Darwin among the machines'. In Weinstock, M. (ed.) *System City: Infrastructure and the Space of Flows*. London: Architectural Design, pp. 66–71.

Sen A. (1989) 'Development as capability expansion', *Journal of Development Planning*, 19, 1: 41–58.

—— (2010) *The Idea of Justice*. London: Penguin.

Sennett, R. (2012) 'The stupefying smart city'. In Burdett, R. and P. Rode (eds.) *Urban Age Electric City Conference*. London: London School of Economics, p. 16.

—— (2013) 'The open city', *mimeo*.

Serres, M. (2012) *Biogea*. Minneapolis: Univocal.

—— (2014) *Times of Crisis. What the Financial Crisis Revealed and How to Reinvent our Lives and Future*. London: Bloomsbury.

Shaviro, S. (2014) *The Universe of Things. On Speculative Realism.* Minneapolis: University of Minnesota Press.

Shepard, M. (ed.) (2011) *Sentient City: Ubiquitous Computing, Architecture, and the Future of Urban Space.* Cambridge, MA: MIT Press.

Silwa, M. and K. Riach (2012) 'Making scents of transition: smellscapes and the everyday in "old" and "new" urban Poland', *Urban Studies*, 49, 1: 23–41.

Simmel, G. (2002) 'The metropolis and mental life'. In Bridge, G. and S. Watson (eds.) *The Blackwell City Reader.* Oxford: Wiley, Blackwell.

Simone, A. (2010) *City Life from Jakarta to Dakar.* New York: Routledge.

—— (2011) 'The surfacing of urfan life', *City*, 15, 3–4: 355–64.

—— (2014a) *Jakarta: Drawing the City Near.* Minneapolis: University of Minnesota Press.

—— (2014b) 'Relational infrastructures in postcolonial urban worlds'. In Graham, S. and C. McFarlane (eds.) (2014) *Infrastructural Lives: Urban Infrastructure in Context.* London: Routledge, pp. 17–38.

Sloterdijk, P. (2011) *Bubbles. Spheres I.* New York: Semiotext(e).

—— (2015) *Stress and Freedom.* Cambridge: Polity.

Smil, V. (2013) *Harvesting the Biosphere. What We Have Taken from Nature.* Cambridge, MA: MIT Press.

Smith, D. W. (1997) 'Introduction' in Gilles Deleuze, *Essays Critical and Clinical.* Minneapolis: University of Minnesota Press, pp. xi–liii.

Sparrow, T. (2013) *Levinas Unhinged.* Alresford, Hampshire: Zero Books.

Steel, C. (2009) *Hungry City. How Food Shapes Our Lives.* London: Vintage.

Stengers, I. (2015) *In Catastrophic Times. Recasting the New Barbarism.* Chicago: Open Humanities Press.

Sterelny, K. (2014) *The Evolved Apprentice. How Evolution Made Humans Unique.* Cambridge, MA: MIT Press.

Storper, M. (2013) *Keys to the City.* Princeton: Princeton University Press.

Storper, M. and A. J. Scott (2016) 'Current debates in urban theory: A critical reassessment', *Urban Studies*, online version March 2016: DOI: 10.1177/0042098016634002.

Storper, M. and A. Venables (2004) 'Buzz, face-to-face contact and the urban economy', *Journal of Economic Geography*, 4: 351–70.

Sturgis, R. C. (2015) *The Mammals That Moved Mankind*. London: Authorhouse.

Suddendorf, T. (2014) *The Gap. The Science of What Separates Us From Other Animals*. New York: Basic Books.

Sundaram, R. (2010) *Pirate Modernity: Media Urbanism in Delhi*. London: Routledge.

Swanton, D. (2010) 'Flesh, metal, road: tracing the machinic geographies of race', *Environment and Planning D: Society and Space*, 28, 3: 447–66.

Tacoli, C., Bukhari, B. and S. Fisher (2013 'Urban poverty, food security and climate change', *Human Settlements Working Paper No 37*, London: International Institute for Environment and Development.

Tantner, A. (2015) *House Numbers. Pictures of a Forgotten History*. London: Reaktion.

Taylor, P. (2004) *World City Network: A Global Urban Analysis*. London: Routledge.

—— (2013) *Extraordinary Cities*. Cheltenham: Edward Elgar.

Thieme, T. (2010) 'Youth, waste and work in Mathare: whose business and whose politics?', *Environment and Urbanization*, 22, 2: 333–52.

—— (2013) 'The "hustle" amongst youth entrepreneurs in Mathare's informal waste economy', *Journal of Eastern African Studies*, 7, 3: 389–412

Thompson, K. (2014) *Where Do Camels Belong? The Story and Science of Invasive Species*. London: Profile Books.

Thrift, N. J. (2007) *Non-representational Theory: Space, Politics, Affect*. London: Routledge.

—— (2012) 'The insubstantial pageant: producing an untoward land', *Cultural Geographies*, 19, 2: 141–68.

—— (2014) 'The "sentient" city and what it may portend', *Big Data and Society*, 1: 1–21.

—— (2015) 'The weight of the world', *Journal of Space Syntax*, 6: 102–3.

Tompkins, D. (2014) 'Weird ecology: on the Southern reach trilogy', *LA Review of Books*, 30 September.

Toomey, D. (2013) *Weird Life. The Search for Life that is Very Different from our Own*. New York: Norton.

Townsend, A. (2013) *Smart Cities*. New York: Norton.

Truelove, Y. and E. Mawdsley (2011) 'Discourses of citizenship and criminality in clean, green Delhi'. In Clark-Decès, I. (ed.) *A Companion to the Anthropology of India*. Oxford: Wiley-Blackwell.

Tsing, A. L. (2015) *The Mushroom at the End of the World. On the Possibility of Life in Capitalist Ruins*. Princeton: Princeton University Press.

UNDP (2010) *Human Development Report 2010: The Real Wealth of Nations*. New York: United Nations Development Programme.

UN-Habitat (2003) *Slums of the World*. Nairobi: United Nations Human Settlements Programme.

—— (2008) *State of the World's Cities 2010/2011: Bridging the Urban Divide*. Nairobi: United Nations Human Settlements Programme.

—— (2011) *Infrastructure for Economic Development and Poverty Reduction in Africa*. Nairobi: United Nations Human Settlements Programme.

—— (2012) *State of the World's Cities 2012/2013: Prosperity of Cities*. Nairobi: United Nations Human Settlements Programme.

—— (2013) *Streets as Public Spaces and Drivers of Urban Prosperity*. Nairobi: United Nations Human Settlements Programme.

Valverde, M. (2011) 'Seeing like a city: the dialectic of modern and premodern ways of seeing in urban governance', *Law and Society Review* 45, 2: 277–312.

—— (2012) *Everyday Law on the Street. City Governance in an Age of Diversity*. Chicago: University of Chicago Press.

—— (2015) *Chronotopes of Law. Jurisdiction, Scale and Governance*. Abingdon: Routledge.

VanderMeer, J. (2014 a, b, c) *Acceptance. Authority. Annihilation*. London: Fourth Estate.

Venkatesh, S. (2014) *Floating City*. New York: Penguin Press.

Vince, G. (2014) *Adventures in the Anthropocene. A Journey to the Heart of the Planet We Made*. London: Chatto and Windus.

Vismann, C. (2008) *Files*. Stanford: Stanford University Press.

Viveiros de Castro, E. (2011) *The Inconstancy of the Indian Soul*. Chicago: Prickly Paradigm Press.

—— (2015) *The Relative Native. Essays on Indigenous Conceptual Worlds*. Chicago: Hau Books.

Walker, R. (2015) 'Building a better theory of the urban', *City*, 2–3: 183–91.

Watts, P. (2014) *Echopraxia*. New York: Tor.

Weinstock, M. (2013) 'Introduction'. In Weinstock, M. (ed.) *System City: Infrastructure and the Space of Flows*. London: Architectural Design, pp. 15–23.

Weizman, E. (2012) *The Least of All Possible Evils*. London: Verso.

World Bank (2009) *Systems of Cities: Harnessing Urbanization for Growth and Poverty Alleviation*. New York: World Bank.

—— (2012) *Transformation through Infrastructure*. Washington: World Bank.

Zalasiewicz, J. (2009) *The Earth After Us: What Legacy Will Humans Leave in the Rocks?* Oxford: Oxford University Press.

Index